THE REVELATION OF
WHY

ISBN-13   Paperback   978-1-967903-89-4
            eBook   978-1-967903-88-7

Library of Congress Control Number: 2025919712

THE REVELATION OF
WHY

NATHANIEL FRAZIER

BOOK DOMAIN LLC

AUTHOR INTRODUCTION

My name is Nathaniel the gift from God. The Revelation of Why is designed to get you to challenge someone else to help you balance your negative and positive character traits. It is a way to gain instant report with people and receive a lift that can help you through your day. This book is the initial foundation of Revelation Why Education. In order to keep your thoughts balanced you must first balance your minds thoughts between the negative character weaknesses and your positive traits. Once there is an equilibrium or balance of these energies, they will attract more like energies which will force change to appear right before your eyes. Let us also agree to help educate as many people as we can about mental warfare that goes on in the minds of many people. I help you discover the origin of "negative character weaknesses" through the Revelation of Why and Revelation Why Education and teach you to balance them (your own negative weaknesses, and the weaknesses of others affecting your life). The Revelation of Why is the result of my own pursuit. I have a Certification in Neuro-Linguistic Programming, served in the Military for 5 years, a Youth Services officer for the State of Tennessee for two and a half years, an Extradition Agent transporting fugitives nationwide for seven and a half years and a Sheriff's Deputy for over 8 years. Throughout my life, I have tried to learn from my mistakes. Well, it seems that since I kept making decisions that I was not happy with or could not stick to, it was time to figure out "why." In addition, this is what brought about the "Revelation of Why." There was a time when my ex-wife and I went through a lot of miscommunications especially when her son past. I did not know what to say to a grieving wife and mother. She was trusting in the Lord to bring her through somehow. It was I that could not continue to bare the miscommunication between her and I. So, after getting divorced I asked God to give me some answers and that is when I was supplied with The Revelation of Why. I asked how can I communicate with anyone that is grieving? You and other humans were created similar, yet totally different beings. The best way that you can effectively communicate with this being is to speak to him or her using their own concepts that are in alignment with their own inner belief systems. Try to get them to write down or express positive trigger words or positive character traits that are used in similar fashion as affirmations. The only difference with these affirmations or trigger words is the fact that they are a product of their own intellect and thought concept that should help to trigger positive impulses stimulating the brain to override the negative emotions. I thank the Creator for giving me insight to the information in this book. It was a profound help to understand why people do what they do. Understanding "Why" is the key to the whole battle. That is because, if you know the why at least you can have an easier time moving forward. Remember you do not have to accept the why, just knowing is half the battle. The rest is up to you and how you respond to the why.

CONTENTS

GLOSSARY OF TERMS

1. Accountability Chart – A chart that allows you the ability to document and tract your character progress.

2. Appreciate – An excited utterance to express unconditional esteem.

3. Cast Members – Cast members are people that directly or indirectly influence your life. These are also people that you have direct contact with whether in conversation in person or by some other forms of communication.

4. Circle of Karma – Within the circle of life you get out of it what you put into it.

5. Desire – The feeling that accompanies an unsatisfied state.

6. Environment – The totality of surrounding conditions.

7. Esoteric Catalyst Phrases (ECP) – Hidden phrases we make up acquire and live by.

8. Esoteric Negative Character Weaknesses (ENCW) – These character weaknesses describe our hidden negative nature as it pertains to our own hidden desires.

9. Esteem – The condition of being honored, respected, or well regarded.

10. Forced Positivity– To force yourself to think positive most of the time and find the positive in the negative.

11. Fun Mental Response List (FMRL) – A precompiled fun list of sarcastic responses used in fun to help sarcastic people.

12. Mental Combat – Various negative character weaknesses engage in a mental battle to see who has the loudest voice in your mind.

13. Negative Thought Default – A tendency to think negative without having to force ourselves.

14. Negative Character Weakness Phrases List– This is a systematic list that you create in sequential order annotating your negative character weaknesses.

15. Positive Character Traits (PCT) or Trigger words – Traits that describe the positive nature of a person.

16. Positive Response List (PRL) – Created positive responses used to encourage purging the heart and balancing negative character weaknesses.

17. Reality Check – Taking your "negative character weaknesses" and using them to describe you to other people without telling them it is you.

18. Regular Negative Character Weaknesses– These are common character weaknesses that describe our general nature as it pertains to our desires.

19. Receiving Celebrity Status – Telling a person up front why you compliment them and get them to beat you saying I appreciate you.

20. Self–diagnoses – An assessment of where your heart is really at in terms of what has priority in your life.

SUMMARY

If you are interested in making changes in your life for the better, you must ask yourself, "Is "why" (the reason I want to change) big enough or worth it?" In other words, are the sacrifices and consequences of your actions worth the *reason why* you should change? I believe that in order to sustain a major change for good in life you must make it personal. Really, it is just a matter of time before "negative character weaknesses" will influence your thoughts to make bad decisions. Remember that whether you want to change or not you have to answer to someone. It is a given that whether you choose to change or not you are not going to please everybody. I believe that this book will offer a wealth of knowledge that will open your eyes to a different way of looking at things. If given a chance, the usage of the techniques in this book will help you make better choices through the "Revelation of Why." The book will give examples of how the technique I call "Forced Positivity" can be beneficial in all situations. The book will show you, your family, and/or friends how to work on your individual "character weaknesses", while having fun and building up trust in a relationship. The book will teach you techniques on how to safeguard your "core belief negative character weaknesses" from other people who are oblivious to the fact that they have a need to feed their negativity. Although, we are all guilty of feeding our need to be negative, the book will show you how to make a positive response list along with a fun mental response list to help combat those "core belief negative character weaknesses."

I will show you how to make a chart that displays each negative character weakness you chose to work on daily. The chart has a negative and a positive side to it. You can compete with another person or by yourself and receive points that tally up at the end of the week or designated time. Whether you win or lose everyone wins, because your character and trust revive itself in a relationship. Since you make up your own list of positive responses you do not have to worry about someone else telling you how to change, when they can recommend you use the concepts, phrases, or positive trigger words that you make up to help you get through problems. By forcing yourself to pick out one or two of your "core belief negative character weaknesses" to work on daily and using as many positive responses you can think of to combat the negative, you will start to purge your heart, which feeds the subconscious. This process may take a while to master, but it will help you make choices that you are a lot happier with, because you are constantly finding positive responses to combat the negative. The book expresses the importance of you being the main character in your life, while you are filming on the set of your "life's story." The book teaches you that you need to respect the various rolls people play in your life. You do not have to agree with them to respect them. You do not have to agree with your enemy, but you should respect them. The book will suggest ways to minimize the ticking time bombs walking around in the world. The techniques in this book are most effective if the people or person is willing to change.

The book will teach you that telling a person "Why" you appreciate that person for being who they are, and not for what they did/do (without conditions) makes that person feel much better and opens the door to other positive responses. If everyone practiced the techniques in this book, the world would be a better place to live in. This book offers you a unique and creative way to soul-search yourself. It allows you to see, if change is really an option for you, and show if you are willing to change or improve your life. You will feel good. This is a new thought to handle an ancient problem. Although these techniques may not be very modern, they are new to this generation.

THE PROCESS OF MAKING BETTER CHOICES IN LIFE

The Revelation of Why will:

1. Give you a technique to help purge the heart, which feeds the subconscious of negative thoughts.
2. Help you make better choices.
3. Give you help in understanding most relationship issues.
4. Teach you how to observe behavior (whether yours or someone else's), process it, and discover how to improve yourself.
5. Teach you to be responsible for the actions that you make before you make them, because you are utilizing a technique that can get you excited if it is applied.
6. Make you aware of things about yourself that you may have mis-understood, which may have a profound effect upon your life or someone else's.

7. Enlighten your approach on life from a very new perspective.

8. Strengthen the weakest link in your personality.

9. Teach you not to focus on other people's problems; but to concentrate on yourself, since you are the one that makes the final decision to act on your thoughts.

10. Encourage you to recognize and observe when you or someone else has a need to feed negativity, and as a result, process which environment negativity is starving the most.

11. Create an accountability chart that you can go back a reference to track your progress.

"REGULAR CORE BELIEF NEGATIVE CHARACTER WEAKNESSES"

These are common character weaknesses that describe our general nature as it pertains to our own desires. Most humans express a lot of these character weaknesses daily.

- pornography
- pride
- discouraged
- rejection
- hatred
- denial
- lack of trust
- frustration
- hurt
- boredom
- unthankful
- fear
- vengeance
- lust
- covet
- wrath
- disappointment
- desire
- impatience
- disrespect
- anger
- no affection
- cold blood
- stealing

- lying
- bragging/ boasting
- yelling
- ruthless
- needy
- procrastination
- lazy
- loneliness
- selfishness
- users/abusers
- no tolerance
- cussing
- grumpy
- envy
- strife
- evil
- spiteful
- nosy
- greedy

More "core belief negative character weaknesses" may be added to the list.

"CORE BELIEF NEGATIVE CHARACTER WEAKNESS PHRASES LIST"

This is a systematic list that you create in sequential order annotating your negative character weaknesses.

- I'm going to get you before you get me.
- You can't teach me anything.
- I don't have to take anything from anyone.
- I can't control myself.
- You can't control me.
- I do what I want to do when I'm good and ready.
- I don't listen to anyone.
- I am easily persuaded.
- I love power and being in control.
- Eye for Eye/This for That.
- The tone of a person's voice.
- You don't correct me.
- You're not my mother or father.
- I tell you what to do.

- Too defensive
- Problems with authority
- Lack of interest
- I don't care if I'm rude.
- I don't care about you.

"ESOTERIC NEGATIVE CHARACTER WEAKNESSES"

These character weaknesses describe our hidden negative nature as it pertains to our own hidden desires. We make these up in our minds and secretly live by them. Below are some examples.

- resentment
- defiance
- unloving
- correction
- short fuse
- corrupt mind
- fault-finding
- rebellion

More "core belief negative character weaknesses" may be added to the list.

"ESOTERIC CATALYTIC PHRASES"

These are hidden phrases we make up acquire and live by. These phrases require some kind of sacrifice. To obtain the coveted results one must be willing to do whatever it takes. One must be willing to endure or even sacrifice their life for their cause or belief. Sometimes a negative esoteric catalyst phrase incurs karmic debt. This is covered in the chapter of the circle of karma.

- I desire to be rich and famous at any cost.
- I desire to have sex at any cost.
- I desire to kill at any cost.
- I desire to be immortal at any cost.
- I desire to be someone else at any cost.
- I desire to serve my God at any cost.
- I desire to save people at any cost.

DESIRE

I believe the ability to fulfill your desire to contribute to the greater good or the desire of another in life's greater good is the most important thing in life after time. The fulfillment of desire can be good if the intent bears a positive result. The want and need that battle for a date with desire goes back to when we were babies and beyond. Babies unknowingly test parent's character weaknesses daily. Babies do this when they want and need food, to be changed and attention. As a baby grows into a childhood their wants and needs grow tremendously. The oblivious child tests many to see, if they will fulfill their wants and needs.

Sometimes a parent neglecting their child's desires influences negative character weaknesses in that child. There is an example of this in the chapter with the skits. There is a scene where Matt's father gives him a puff of his cigarette at the age of six. Matt's father is fulfilling his desire to smoke and drink alcohol while watching television. When Matt asks his father for another puff, he refuses to consider Matt's wants and needs now that he has influenced him to smoke.

As we grow into adulthood the oblivious testing and exposing of character progresses. As the want and need grows, so does the desire to have it. People can allow the conquest of fulfillment consume them in everything they do. I am not trying to say desire is a bad thing. I am saying consider carefully the intent and the long-term possibilities that come with it. With some desires once, you cross that line there is no turning back.

Many will find out that the fulfillment of some extreme negative desires incurs a karmic debt. I cover this in the chapter on the Circle of Karma later in this book. A healthy dose of desire can do a body, career, life, and others some good.

The lines that separate good and bad desires can appear grey and hazy. One's focus on what they desire can overwhelm them so, that the consequences do not matter. Esoteric Catalyst Phrases will surely test everything you have in you. Ask yourself; have you intended to fulfill any of the esoteric catalyst phrases? If your answer is yes, then you have drawn a clear line of intention. The main factor that draws the line is at any cost. Next ask yourself does the want and need reflect what is in my heart. This is very important if you want to avoid regret later.

When a person maintains anger in them, they desire to feed the need to be negative. Whether desire is good or bad it has a need to feed to survive. This is why I am not surprised when I see or hear so much negativity in the world. I do not agree with it; however, I understand it. I mentioned this in the beginning of the book. I believe that no matter who or what you are, your negative character weaknesses receive a daily dose of testing. I think test exist to improve our character and try to maintain a proper balance of character weaknesses and positive traits. I believe the human race and all in existence displays desire.

INTRODUCTION TO THE REVELATION OF WHY

This book is an attempt to reveal to you some "negative character weaknesses" influencing your thoughts to make bad choices. This is an opportunity to free you from the old way of thinking. The techniques in this book will show you a new way of thinking that works on removing limitations in your mind. It teaches you to say no to the desire to utilize an excuse to achieve what you want in life that requires a negative result. You have the Free Will to "put chains on the brain", creating new limitations that keep you bound up, unable to be who or what you were meant to be. Unbound the chains of limiting beliefs that focus on negative reality and focus one ones of positive reality. Until people realize "why" in the way people react and respond to problems and situations being influenced by esoteric negative /regular "negative character weaknesses" from their childhood, friends, and most relationships, they will continue experiencing the same results.

We will not know the answer to all of the why questions, but the ones we can receive answers to will help keep things moving a lot smoother in life. I believe that one important factor among many in determining how you respond to a problem or situation is how you accept, understand or refuse "why" in that problem or situation. The next important factor that influences your "why" is your "negative character weaknesses."

Since most of these weaknesses are deeply rooted in the heart from our childhood, it is not an easy task to want to deal with them, especially since we tend not to realize we are using them. These "negative character weaknesses" put limitations on how you respond to problems or situations. They put limitations on how far you will succeed in life and whether you will allow yourself to be happy in life. They also put limitations on whom you are willing to deal with and how long you are willing to entertain what they have to say. This is because your thought processes are set on certain emotions that are awakened by your negative character weaknesses. One can cast the blame on demons influencing their thoughts and that is up to them. It is my belief system that These demons are made of negative energy and if you choose to paint a red negative stain in your brain that is negative and refuse to wash it out or remove it, then you may be attracting unwanted energy that you might not want to remain in your life. These "negative character weaknesses" set off a chain reaction in the brain stimulating other "negative character weaknesses" to fire off, which influences our thoughts. Rarely will you only find one negative character weakness exposed when a problem or situation arises. In like manner when you work on your positive character traits, they set off other positive character traits, which allow you a chance to work on more of them.

There are helpful scripts that you will need to memorize in this book. For example, if you are working on your cursing, the very moment that you leak out a curse word, if you are a religious person, God is not first on your mind at that moment. If you are not a religious person, without memorizing a positive response you will allow your "negative character weaknesses" to influence your thoughts and curse anyway. This book addresses a critical need that, if left unchecked, will lead to society getting more than it can handle. This book will teach you how to keep from stressing or worrying about things that you cannot change. I will teach you how to understand the process of making better choices through the "Revelation of Why", which is the process you should use daily as to not focus so much on the person, problem, or situation, but instead, focus on your inner-self at the time you experience negative thoughts. People who choose to dwell and focus their attention on another person, problem, or circumstance, have elected by their actions to place limitations on how long they will be able to be helped. As soon as someone offers some relief they eventually go back to dwelling on their "negative character weaknesses", which influences their thoughts. This can be a clear example of the stain in the brain that I mentioned earlier. This explains "why" some people cannot be helped that does not have a mental disorder. You do not have to agree with what or how the cast member, situation or problem presents itself, just as long as you understand "why" it is doing "what" it is doing. People with mental disorders suffer with the same problem as well, besides their chemical imbalance in the brain or even other factors. How close you are to God and your education will not mean anything if your thoughts are on your "negative character weaknesses." In most cases, Free Will is taken for granted, when in reality the Free Will to choose to work on your "negative character weaknesses" can have a tremendous impact on the choices you make, how far you will go in life, if happiness is even possible, and the ability to learn the core reasons "why" people do what they do. If you can accept "why" in anything in life, you can move forward a lot easier.

THE EXPLANATION OF THE REVELATION OF WHY

I planned a trip to Gulf Port Mississippi for my ex-wife and me. As soon as I booked the hotel for a Friday and Saturday night, I realized that I still had to work Friday and would not get off work until 11pm. I called the place where I made the reservation to cancel one of the dates and the operator informed me, "I can't find you in the system." It is a good thing I was working on balancing my "negative character weaknesses." To make things worse, by mistake, I pushed the "trash" icon on my iPhone and accidentally deleted the email. The booking agent asked me for my email address and then told me that she could not find it in the system either. Fortunately, I wrote down the confirmation number and I was able to give that to her. My old self would have blown up and expressed myself in a way that I would have regretted. I knew from booking the room the first time that they said that the hotel was almost entirely booked.

The woman I talked to said that I needed to book another room first, before she would transfer me over to her cancellation department. This meant I had to use another credit card to book this room because I did not have enough on the other card. Keep in mind, now my wife is expecting us to go to Gulf Port. I cannot afford to miss booking this room. While trying not to focus on the problem and by balancing my "negative character weaknesses" (anger, frustration, pride, and impatience) I was able to improve my positive character traits. By utilizing the technique of "Forced Positivity," applying trust and faith, I was able to get my money back and get a hotel room booked for the day I needed. Anyone can say that all you needed is trust in the LORD. In order for me to exercise the trust, I needed to make the hotel book in happen, then I had to balance out the "negative character weaknesses" inside first in order for me to make a better, informed choice through the "Revelation of Why."

I could have elected to feed my need to be negative, only to look forward to getting into a prolonged argument with my wife over me not booking the hotel room. However, when I look back, I was happy that I balance out my "negative character weaknesses" and applied "Forced Positivity." My wife and I had a wonderful trip. I did not have to use the booking agent as a scapegoat to cover for me neglecting to work on my "negative character weaknesses," which were pride, anger, trust, and impatience. You still must use sound judgment with situations like these, because a scammer trying to take my money as well could have fooled me.

You have to open your mind and view cast members and problems from the standpoint that they are just doing their job on the set of your life's story, which is to work on your "negative character weaknesses" for free. I believe that each individual is their own main character in their own show or movie in life and everyone else is just cast members. This is because you cannot change or fix other people; they have to want to change on their own. Since you are responsible for you, it is your job in your show to work on building your character. The Free Will that you were given allows you to be the director and main character of your movie in your life. In this book, you will be introduced to some helpful scripts that you will need to memorize. This is on the set of your life while filming and interacting with other cast members. The filming of your life's story is more of a metaphor comparing it to the similarities in a movie. All of the filming is in your thoughts and in your mind. There are different roles one can play, but in your life, you should be the main character. Cast members are people that directly interact with you as the main character or indirectly have an impact on decisions or help influence your decisions in your movie called life. Extras are the fill-in people in the background in your movie that are doing their own thing, keeping busy. Instead of watching movies on TV all the time, take charge of the leading role in your own movie. Do something extraordinary to change someone else's life or your own. When you find yourself alone and getting down on yourself, because you are operating on a low budget film in your life, you should seek or call on the one or the thing that gives you strength and apply "Forced Positivity."

It is one thing to understand that cast members work on your "negative character weaknesses" for free, but a very different ball game when that environment awakens extreme voices. When the mental combat from the extreme voices is on the battlefield it is like the battle with bows, arrows, swords, and chariots have left the field and now we are using modern weapons of warfare. The modern weapons are far more destructive than the ones in the past. This is where your mind may battle over harming yourself, others, or other things because negativity has a need to feed to find some relief. I have experienced driving down the road to "destination nowhere" with an estimated time of arrival "whenever the mental combat in my mind stops". I was in my car driving down the road experiencing what I call extreme mental combat from my environment. All it would take is to have a disgruntle driver provoke me while driving and experiencing extreme mental warfare to act on the loudest voice at that moment. While my esoteric "negative character weaknesses" battled my regular "negative character weaknesses" for the loudest voice, the battle was joined by negative character phrases voicing their option. The negative character phrase that keeps leading the charge was "you don't have to take anything from anyone." My father instilled this phrase in me when I was very young. Since my mind was full of confusion from the extreme mental warfare going on, I made things worse by clinging to the negative character phrases that kept me in bondage. The negative character phrases placed limitations on who I would allow to help me, what I was willing to entertain from what someone had to say, and if happiness was an option in my life. Fortunately, someone called looking for me while I was driving and realized that something was wrong.

This person managed to negotiate a cease-fire of the mental warfare. One of the hardest (and loudest) voices I had to contend with, which was contrary to my negative character phrase, was: "Why are you always running from people, problems, or situations that do not go your way?" In many cases, the potential to work out a problem or situation is great. However, when you find yourself entering the extreme mental combat zone it is best to remove yourself from that environment. You must also be careful removing yourself, because it increases the possibility of becoming a victim of increased circumstance when you enter different environments. You may not be paying attention to the fact that although you are out of that environment, you have a need to feed your negativity. This is when you seek out someone else to expose his or her "negative character weaknesses" by saying something smart or negative to feed your own need. You could also decide to become a predator and prey on innocent people because you never got past "why" you were treated the way you were treated. You should never underestimate the mental combat that another person is going through just because you feel that your mental combat is greater. Know your limits and stick to them or you may find yourself making an even worse decision than staying in that environment. To elect not to do anything about your "negative character weaknesses" is like watching erosion come on untreated metal over time. At first everything is strong but left neglected will begin to erode away and become useless. In like manner, if you chose to disregard your "negative character weaknesses" you will experience problems in your relationships whether platonic or intimate.

Your supervisor may pass you up on jobs and promotions. If you broke your leg or your arm, you would have to go through physical therapy. As a part of your recovery, you will have to endure a lot of pain. This concept is the same with working on "negative character weaknesses". While you are working on your character weaknesses, you will not always want to do what it takes to strengthen your character weaknesses, because it can be mentally painful or embarrassing. However, if you stick to the techniques in this book you will find that you will strengthen all of your character weaknesses that you work on and receive the desired results. The results that you are striving to obtain are strengthening your positive character traits and balance your negative ones. This will allow you to be able to make better-informed choices without the influence of your "negative character weaknesses" causing you to decide that you may not want to live with later.

You are exposed to many "negative character weaknesses" throughout life. If left unchecked or not worked on, the result is bad decision-making and regret. If you have a short fuse and problems with impatience, you must address it constantly and on a daily basis. It will not matter who or what is before you at your time of need. You will begin to get upset and radical thoughts will begin to sprout and take root in your mind. In that end, you find yourself doing or saying something that you wish you would have taken a little more time to put more thought into or had more patience. As an example: If you have a problem with not caring enough, it will be just a matter of time before the one you claim you love does something that upsets you and that negative character weakness kicks in protect mode and you are out the door. You may be looking for another relationship or not wanting to help that person. The problem with this negative character weakness is it does not really matter who or which mate you are in a relationship with, as soon as they upset you, the not caring mechanism kicks in protective mode and now anything goes. Of course, there are many potential responses, but these are just a few.

A problem gives your inner-self a chance to expose a variety of "negative character weaknesses" that dwell within you. People who commit murder and other crimes have chosen not to work on their "negative character weaknesses". They act on their "negative character weaknesses" that influence their thoughts, which place limitations in their mind as to finding the best possible solutions to their problem. I believe most of the time people that commit crimes are oblivious to the fact that their own "negative character weaknesses" are the main source of origin that influences them to commit these acts. Which brings us to the question why? Although there could be many reasons a person does what he/she does, to me the origin of the problem remains the same. For example, if a person was in jail for a crime that they committed, they may accept the fact that they did it, because they knew they did wrong. They may not agree with the fact that they were caught, but because they understood the why they were arrested; they had an easier time going to jail or prison than, then if they had not committed a crime. They understood that the police officer was doing his job. That is the why he or she was arrested. If in the same situation, a man tried to arrest a man without a uniform, badge or gun, the person that committed the crime would not accept being arrested by that person even though they committed a crime. The person that committed the crime will not accept being arrested because the arresting person does not have the authority to arrest the criminal. Likewise, the person would not accept the why they were arrested by a civilian. You do not have to agree with the job that a person is doing, but if you can accept the why a person is doing what they are doing then you can move forward, thus proving the fact that if you cannot get past "why" you will have a hard time moving forward in life.

The world is full of ticking time bombs waiting to go off at a moment's notice to defend their thoughts, actions, and ways. Some of the manifestations of a ticking time bomb, engaged in mental warfare by you or someone else, are when a person is upset about something and comes to you to either expose your "negative character weaknesses" or vent to release theirs.

Something to consider is they smile in your face and say what you want to hear, but helping you is not in their heart. People will verbally display "negative character weaknesses" like, anger, frustration, wrath, resentment etc. A conversation could be going well and all of a sudden, the person you are talking with explodes after something you said that triggered the mental warfare. A person all of a sudden gets quiet after you mention something to them. Some things that could trigger the mental warfare are religion, politics, race, gender, the need to feed, unaddressed esoteric "negative character weaknesses", regular "negative character weaknesses", "esoteric catalyst phrases" and "negative character phrases".

It might seem obvious that the reason why a person robbed you was lack of money; however, I think that it goes deeper than that. If the negative character weakness of desire and coveting were not present in the heart, the person would have found another means to get the money. The same is true with other crimes as well.

You have to force yourself to dwell on positive responses that you make up to combat the mental warfare going on in your mind. Dwelling on positive responses is the work that is required for you to do, if you want to move forward in life without allowing only "negative character weaknesses" to influence your thoughts and bring forth mental balancing.

RELATIONSHIPS

If "why" is the result of what happens in a relationship, focus on those "negative character weaknesses" in yourself and work on them instead of focusing on the problems that exists between you and your mate. This is not to say you need to forget about your problem at hand. For example, if you are in love with your mate and he or she is causing you continual stress with something that they are doing, ask them to try the techniques in this book with you, together. If you both work on your internal issues at the same time, both of you will become more aware of your "negative character weaknesses" that help influence your thoughts. You will receive more understanding of one another. You and your mate will feel like you both are caring for each other's feelings. By doing these both of you will not, have to ask why or what the other person is doing to improve the relationship. Instead, you will have a better appreciation for "why" by just knowing before something happens. Keeping track with the accountability chart will help you with a new problem that might surface. You will have a better idea of what your mate or cast member is already going through. Having a chart to refer to will remind you about how your mate is feeling the day before, which could spill over into the next day.

It will only take one day for you to begin to strengthen or reduce your "negative character weaknesses," but you will witness positive results immediately when you do. By possessing this knowledge ahead of time, you can make better choices and it will help you learn more about yourself and your mate. If you chose not to write the character weaknesses down and look at them daily with yourself and for your mate, you will only focus on the main issues that stick out in your mind. It might be the same "negative character weaknesses" that you continually fail to work on, because you did not write it down or see it as a problem. These may be the main problems that your mate is experiencing with you. Each day you and your mate fill in the negative character weakness list and then share your list with each other. Never fill in a list of character weakness for your mate without permission from him or her, because they have to agree to work on the character weaknesses that are on his or her list to improve them and not you. Only you can take responsibility for yourself and change. I believe we humans are hotwired to believe in our own concepts that we perceive we make up. Then ask each other, how you can help me work on these issues today. You can help support each other by encouraging each other to use the positive responses from your list to handle every problem or situation that you encounter with each other.

If you find that you are getting into a heated discussion, agree to take a break or each one expresses their views and when you are finished, agree to be done with that conversation and not bring it up again. Both of you will be moving forward in your relationship and can concentrate on working on character weaknesses that are on your lists. Take deep breaths and let it out easy, if you are stressing. If your mate is doing something you do not like and you feel in your heart, he or she is testing you by asking you what is wrong, tell him or her with a smile, "I'm just working on me." Remember your mate or cast member is just doing their job, which is to expose your "negative character weaknesses" for free and you must recognize that. Understand that most people do not like working for free. That being said, when someone is working my nerves, I have been known to ask them, how does it feel to be working my nerves for free? If they try to be smart and say, "it's not work I enjoy it," they apparently either do not realize or they do not care that their negative character weaknesses with desire are controlling their actions without them believing or knowing it. The mental warfare in that mind is so intense that any excuse will do, because the negativity has a need to feed whether they like it or not. By working on internal issues, that you feel will help your relationship and discussing each other's character weakness from the list you make each day, your mate can help you work on your issues if you are going through a tough time. You will find that this technique will build trust, transparency and a better understanding of you and your partner's issues. No matter what the topic, issue or problem is if "why" is not accepted, understood or you have your own created explanation for "why," it will be difficult for a person to move forward in life at a pace that is acceptable to them or society.

Couples that are sincere about working on a relationship, but constantly feel like they are on a roller coaster, are focusing more time on spending time together than on balancing their own "negative character weaknesses, "individually. "Negative character weaknesses" are the reason they are on the roller coaster in the first place. For example, if one person in a relationship has the negative character weakness "yelling" (when angry), spending time together will not matter as much to the person receiving the tongue-lashing. You can spend all the time you want going places and doing things to improve the relationship, but until you balance some "negative character weaknesses," you are just setting yourself up for another ride on the roller coaster at some point in the relationship. While one of you (or both of you) think that he/she is doing something for the relationship by planning to go to events, in actuality they are setting themselves up, unknowingly, to get into an argument in public. This is because he or she has never addressed the negative character weakness of yelling and will carry that weakness into another environment in the holster of their mind waiting to go off at a moment's notice to defend his or her thoughts.

Remember, when a person is yelling at you, they are not talking to you but talking at you. If a person is mad at you and yelling, their respect for you just went out the window and disrespect just stepped in a says, "you in my hut now." Depending on how well disrespect is winning or losing a verbal mental contest, it may awaken other "negative character weaknesses" to feed its need to be negative. When the other negative character weakness enters the battlefield, they also have a need to feed. This is one reason why people do what they do, and then wonder why they did what they did. If nothing is wrong with yelling at each other, try yelling at a prominent figure you respect. I believe you will think twice about yelling at a person you respect, if yelling is a part of what people are supposed to do to each other. If it is not a good idea to yell at a prominent figure, why is it ok to yell at the one that you claim you love? Just because you know or do not know the prominent figure does not make it right to yell at him or her. If that is true then, you definitely do not need to yell at the one that you claim you love just because you can. It does not make it right to utilize an excuse to yell at a family member just because they are family. All you are doing is causing mental combat in that family member's head and contributing to the ticking time bombs walking around waiting to go off at a moment's notice to defend their thoughts. That being said, do not get me wrong there are many parts in the world were talking loudly is normal, but when asked, those same loud people can distinguish the difference between a person that is talking loudly and a person that is yelling. I know this first hand because I am originally from Philadelphia Pa. Most people who have anger problems have power and control issues. Usually, the person with the anger and control problems will not feel that they need to work on their weaknesses, because it may make them feel like they are in less control and will not be able to have things done their way. It is hard to have a give and take relationship, if one person does not work on the power and control problem.

In most cases, I have found they are probably in denial about it. Like a weapon in our hand, some of our "negative character weaknesses" are out in plain sight in our facial expressions and other times they are in the holster of our subconscious mind, waiting to be summoned at a moment's notice to defend our thoughts. I suggest that people who have short fuses should work on that before anything. I feel this way because I envision them as people walking around with a pilot light on in their mind waiting for someone or thing to ignite the mental warfare, which heats up the more hostile "negative character weaknesses." I also feel that people with short fuses are like the old cars back in the day with a carburetor that always seems to be stuck on running high. Once a person has been aware of the mental warfare that goes on in yourself and a normal loved one's mind, they should understand that the chances of warfare going on in another people's mind is probably great. This is because nobody grew up in a perfect environment and if they were; for sure some other environments they may have attached themselves to were not perfect and may have caused them to adopt "negative character weaknesses." Many people that do not know you very well are at a disadvantage. This is because they have no idea about mental combat going on in their head. Mental combat is covered in a later chapter of this book. Some relationships like; parent-child or siblings have some idea about you and what upsets you. The chapter on skits later in this book shows Matt's teachers as acquaintances. They have no idea about what is going on in Matt's mind. Without a want or a need, the conversation quickly goes nowhere. This does not matter if the person has to leave the area or not.

In the first skit, schoolteacher Mr. Jacob's tells Matt to go to class. However, since Mr. Jacob's conversation did not supply Matt's want or need, he ignored what Mr. Jacob's first asked. When Mr. Jacobs told Matt, he would call Matt's parents; Matt processes the need to talk to Mr. Jacobs. Matt expounds why he does not want Mr. Jacobs to call his parents. Matt's need is for Mr. Jacobs to reconsider calling his parents.

I have found that the want and the need dictate how you desire to express yourself. For example, some people while having dinner may touch legs under the table to express affection and desire. The fulfillment of what one wants speaks volumes in any conversation and in most situations. You may have wondered why you keep on making bad choices when it comes to picking a mate. Just because your parents may have done the same thing, you may feel like it is hereditary. I think it is you allowing your esoteric "negative character weaknesses" influence your thoughts. For example: if you have a problem with sensitivity, which is an esoteric character weakness and you also have a problem with the tone of a person's voice, which is also an esoteric negative character weakness, then it will not matter who the mate is, you are going to have issues with that person at some point. This is especially true when the other person makes you feel like they are disrespecting you or talking down to you. With that being said, you should not take mental abuse from a person that outright refuses to respect you and yells at you because they are angry. A real friend is very hard to come by these days. Does your friend test and expose his or her character weaknesses on you? When a friend or foe imposes their will on you, they test and expose their character. Sometimes it is intentional and sometimes it is not. You do not have to agree with the testing or exposing. Just understand why it is being done and forward progress is easier to achieve.

Later in the skits chapter Matt realizes why he talks to his best friend the way he does. Matt's best friend Sam may not like how he talks to him. However, because of Sam's relationship with Matt he accepts the why Matt sounds the way he does. This does not mean that Sam likes how Matt sounds. Sam has rationalized to his self why Matt is the way he is. In doing so, Sam can move forward in their relationship. A foe brings a real test of your character. In many cases, a foe will push you to the limits of your ability. A foe can really show you where you are weak. A foe can do the homework of revealing your character weaknesses without charge. After all it is part of the foes job to exploit any weaknesses in you. A foe will do this to gain an advantage over you. You do not have to appreciate or agree with the foe just understand the "why."

Unfortunately, all of our esoteric negative/regular "negative character weaknesses" (along with negative character phrases) get a free ride into every environment. Some people can balance them on a daily basis, while others cannot get past "why."

MENTAL COMBAT

Mental Combat is when various negative character weakness engages in a mental battle to see who has the loudest voice in your mind. I believe whether we want to or not all humans engage in mental combat. Some engage in mental combat more than others do. This is because we all have weaknesses in our character. Most people cannot stand daily testing in the area of character weakness. This may cause unneeded physical or mental stress. Unfortunately, without testing in your area of weakness how can you improve it? Every time a person problem or situation arises, ask yourself what are you trying to tell me about myself? If you focus more on the person or the problem mental combat enters the battlefield. The duration of the battle depends on how many negative characters weakness enter the battle for desire. These voices are what influence our thoughts to do bad things. You can find a list of combatants in earlier list at the beginning of the book. Combatants are esoteric negative character weaknesses, regular negative character weaknesses, negative character phrases, and esoteric catalyst phrases. A mental description of these weaknesses battling each other in the mind is in the chapter with skits. One of the major problems with mental combat is the combatants have a need to feed. When most people experience this, they do not think about it in that sense. They simply give into the need or the want at the time, without deep thought. Deep thought too many times requires patience, which many do not have. I have found that the best way to deal with mental combat is to utilize the accountability chart mentioned earlier in this book. When you use the chart, you chose to work on your character. This in turn will make you a better person. Utilizing the techniques in this book will show you how to balance your negative character traits. The techniques and the chart will give you ammunition to fight each test with confidence.

The battle in the mind rages on: "Who has the loudest voice?" when it has a need to feed negativity. I consider this "mental combat". Another negative character weakness that usually gets the blame is desire. However, in many cases when you ask a person why they chose to do what they did, they do not really know. This is because the initial cause, which was sensitivity, was defeated by the other louder negative character voices in the subconscious. Desire, people, environment, time, and place are critical to helping influence their thoughts. These factors will help determine whether a person will work on or balance their negative character weakness. Many people who have chosen to give up on life have done the same thing. They have not elected to take on the leading actor role in their life's movie and have allowed the esoteric "negative character weaknesses" to infiltrate their thoughts, which influences their decisions. The main person or people directly affecting their life's movie have chosen not to work on themselves and at the same time causing undue heartache and unwanted stress.

If you chose to remain in a hostile environment one of the things that you have done, without thinking about it, was allowed your ticker to start in that environment and continue into another one, because negativity has a need to feed. This also increases the chances of you being a victim of someone else's mental warfare. This is because you will act on the loudest voice that feeds your need to be negative by saying something smart or being a perpetrator who victimizes someone to satisfy your need to feed. You can change the environment, influence the environment in a positive way, balance the "negative character weaknesses" that are influencing the environment, if you choose.

ENVIRONMENTS: SOUL SEARCHING

Many people have used the saying, "I have to do some soul-searching," when in reality they do not know where to begin. This book supplies people with the necessary tools to conduct a personality scan. It will help to identify how to address the "negative character weaknesses" which influence their thoughts, which can set limitations on who we deal with, how far we will go in life, and if we will truly be happy in life. The ultimate goal is to assess and process a problem or situation while balancing out "negative character weaknesses", so that you can make the best-informed decision that you will not regret later. In this chapter you will observe, process, and evaluate just how serious you are about making changes in you. This will help you figure out what is feeding your need for you to stay the way you are. This will help you figure out what is more important to you and if change is even an option. Write down a list of all the circles and environments you surround yourself in. For example:

- School Environment.
- Work Environment.
- Home Environment.
- Organizational Environment.
- Acquaintances Environment.
- Neighborhood Environment.
- Friends Environment.
- Any Clubs you joined.
- Group Environment.

You can add more environments that are specific to you.

Now make a list of all the "negative character weaknesses" you have observed in them. Then make a list of all the "negative character weaknesses" you have adopted from being exposed to them. Ask yourself are these "negative character weaknesses" helping me or placing limitations on me in any way.

Go through each of the list that you just made and make a list of common "negative character weaknesses" from those other lists.

Now compare those lists to your original list of "negative character weaknesses".

You see, anyone can easily say they are going to change and truly mean it, but if you do not recognize the fact that in certain environments you choose to work on your "negative character weaknesses" and in others you refuse. This is because the environment that you choose not to balance your "negative character weaknesses" has a greater influence on your subconscious. This is why your focus is not on you changing you, but on the environment or circle you are involved in. I am not suggesting that you get out of whatever group, organization, or environment you are involved in, however I am suggesting that you balance the "negative character weaknesses" on your list that is feeding your need for you to be the way you are, if you want to change. If you have the ability to influence the environment for the better influencing positive responses to combat the negative ones, then do so. You are kidding yourself, if you think you can change you going in and out of various circles and environment not being consistent and balancing your "negative character weaknesses" only when it is convenient for you. Whichever, circle or environment that you gravitate to with a passion, will more than likely have the loudest voice of influence engaging the subconscious. This is because the desire to be a part of something you are passionate about justifies, then influences the subconscious after permeating the heart. Now that desire is in the subconscious, whichever, "negative character weaknesses" exposed from those environments they get a free pass, because they are justified. It is also true that this may not apply to all people as well. Many times, people will ignore the fact that a certain environment or circle is not helping them balance their "negative character weaknesses", because their esoteric "negative character weaknesses" have never been balanced. Be on the lookout for negativity, it is a consuming fire that wants to ignite and consume everything in its path. It could start as just venting and then go south quickly. A person may try to use what you have in common with them to entice you at first to lure you in and then, slow cook you and before you know it, you are done feeding off his or her negativity. To negativity, the mission was accomplished. So many people do not have a clue that they are set a blaze, engulfed in negativity and that being that way is just a way of life.

One way to help morale in the work place is to grade new employees on how well they handle correction. Correction is an esoteric negative character weakness that is linked to being teachable. You may find that through teaching someone something new, you will more than likely compete with the mindset of a person not wanting to change or that desires to do things their way. Since this is a high probability, you are also likely to expose a person's esoteric negative character weakness in correction without them even noticing it. When a person refuses to receive correction, the response is obvious. They respond with a negative response or negative expression on their face. Sometimes they use body language in the form of moving around. They are trying to act as if they are looking for something or trying to find something, while they are secretly trying to disguise their facial expression. In some cases, they may be able to hide it, but when a problem or person exposes that esoteric negative character weakness it will set off a chain reaction activating the other regular "negative character weaknesses". Their thoughts influence negatively, which answers the reason why some people respond negatively when receiving correction. Unfortunately, this leads to one of the causes of lack of moral among many other reasons. This negative behavior breeds more negativity. Some without realizing it feed their need to be negative by seeking out others to expose their negative character that maybe dormant, but now awakened by the negative character of the one starving to feed their need to be negative. What do you do when confronted with a person that is starving and has to feed their need to be negative? Do you give in and help supply their need while they are exposing your "negative character weaknesses" that you are possibly? working on? On the other hand, do you realize what they are doing and choose to respond with one of your positive character responses or "Forced Positivity"? You can take advantage of any problem that exist and use it to expose your internal "negative character weaknesses." Do this each day by filling out the *negative character weakness list* and become more aware of yourself and your surroundings. I observed a young man make two whole deli sandwiches on hoagie rolls. A customer asked if he was a new employee at the store, and with a smart attitude he said, "Yeah, I've been here about a month." He was quick to defend himself by saying that he has been working there longer than the other two new people. The customer tried to tell him how to make his sandwich, but the proud cocky young man would only accept what he wanted to hear from the customer. In short, he made the sandwich in a way that aggravated the customer and jeopardized future business dealings. If some "negative character weaknesses" are not balanced in some employees, they could cost some businesses owners a lot of money long-term. This also applies in other settings such as schools.

Do not fool yourself into thinking that when you yell at your child, when you are correcting them; and by them being quiet that they are just showing you respect. In some cases, it truly is the case however, in too many cases the lack of response from a child, is really resentment building inside. I am trying to help people to want to talk about the why they are the way they are. Too many people were not allowed to talk freely to their parents about their feelings without receiving some form of retribution. It is not a good thing to raise a child up into adulthood oblivious as to whether they resent you or not. What you fail to realize is that when that child becomes an adult and you find yourself trying to reach out and help that child, too many times, they take advantage of you. This is because resentment in the esoteric phrase was never addressed. After resentment exits the heart and enters the subconscious the need to feed the negativity is great.

Let us go a little deeper into the "Revelation of Why." I believe that keeping weeds out of your soil is mandatory if you want a pretty lawn or garden. In like manner so is dealing with problems and "negative character weaknesses." Open your mind and consider this thought. Weeds that grow in the soil at first are unseen, but time and environmental elements can increase the growth. Consider the metaphor of soil being your mind and the weeds being your "negative character weaknesses." Problems represent environmental elements. Although you may plant in a greenhouse, the outside elements like temperature, heat, ice, wind, and rain have a lot of influence on the soil outside. In this metaphor, the outside elements represent potential problems that exist. As Mother Nature influences the outside soil (or your mind), it exposes or helps germinate your "negative character weaknesses." The fresh plants that are planted, protected, and cultivated inside the greenhouse are the positive character traits or trigger words that you created in your list. Understand that potential problems will always be there. Every human being on earth, born and raised differently, presents a hidden potential problem. The loss of loved ones is also an uncontrollable problem. You must ask yourself which character weakness it is working on. Is it faith, self-control, love, or anger etc.? We must also understand that missed loved ones are cast members too, and you have to focus on you the main character and not the loss. I am not saying that you have to forget the lost loved one, just not focus or dwell on their death. This is because dwelling on things you have no control of has a way of eroding away the positive thoughts that can help you move forward in life. We have no control over the people that come and go in our movie, but we can control how we handle our loss. Failure to process this and work on your "negative character weaknesses" could place limitations on you. People who do not want weeds in their lawn or garden must be proactive by utilizing some form of weed-killer on a regular basis, in order to keep out the weeds. In the same way, you must be proactive, balancing your "negative character weaknesses," which influence your thoughts on a daily basis. Learn to recognize the problems when they manifest themselves. Then you can ask yourself "why is this problem trying to stress me out?" Then you must say, "I got you figured out," "you are trying to expose my "negative character weaknesses", so that I can make a bad decision." You must also say, "I see you are doing your job exposing my "negative character weaknesses"," but only if I give into them. Then you say, "I recognize which negative character weakness you are trying to expose" and tell the problem or cast member in your mind" "It is my job not to let you win or excel at your job." "Is that all you got?" "I can do better than that by showing you that I refuse to let my "negative character weaknesses" influence my decision in this area today." I will just utilize some of my positive responses and "Forced Positivity" to deal with this situation and keep pressing on.

Remember not to focus blame on the cast member or the problem, because they are just doing their job, like the officer in the earlier example. Try not to allow people, problems or situations simmer in your mind. Since what you feed your mind is what you become, it is very important to concentrate on feeding it positive responses to combat the "negative character weaknesses" in the heart. You must also remember, if the problem is something you have no control over, do not allow some negative character weakness like worry, anger, wrath, denial, and rage consume your thoughts. Instead, ask yourself, can you stop Mother Nature from unleashing herself? Recognize which negative character weaknesses are being exposed. Write it down or check it off your list, find positive responses, work on it and make a better-informed decision. Practice "flipping the script" on problems in your life and use them to your advantage. It is a whole lot easier accepting instruction from someone who has been there and done that, than someone who has not been through anything. I am sure you are not the first or the last person to go through some problem that you have no control over. Evaluate and process the problem, learn from it, and help someone else understand how to process making better choices through the "Revelation of Why."

You are the judge and jury as to how well you have done with this open-book test of life. Only you can tell if you are truly making progress. Grading yourself is an ongoing thing throughout your life's story and you are subject to have good and bad days. I feel that in order to achieve the highest grades in this life, you have to make good choices that reflect good moral behavior. You must also become a value producer or a value creator to help this world be a better place.

There is no challenge to submitting your will to negativity. Be strong and courageous, stand up to negativity, and fight it. This course of action might mean that you may have to remove yourself from an environment and seek a positive one. This might mean encouraging a loved one to get this book and the separate workbook as well.

REALITY CHECK

One good way to gauge whether your weaknesses are bad or needs to die if you are not sure, is to conduct a reality check. Taking your "negative character weaknesses" and using them to describe you to people without telling them it is you. This should be done with cast members outside your realm of influence. You can evaluate yourself after you compile your list and ask yourself about the same "negative character weaknesses" as if it were someone else. How would you help someone else with the same "negative character weaknesses"? You see we humans have an easier time making suggestions to help others with the same problem we have. During this process, you can be your own evaluator and suggest positive responses for you, while you are really thinking you are helping someone else. I believe that people who commit murder and crime have chosen by their actions to refuse to work on their "negative character weaknesses" and allow their need to feed negativity influence their thoughts. I believe most people are oblivious to the understanding of the why people make bad choices in life like, murder and crime and just making bad decisions. They have to recognize that the origin of these bad choices originates from their "negative character weaknesses" that are influencing their thought. We constantly pick up "negative character weaknesses" from youth at home, friends, Internet, work environment, TV, and video games. We carry them around in the backpack of our minds into every environment waiting for some person, problem, or situation to expose them and we respond acting on the "negative character weaknesses" with the loudest voice. All this is done without offloading them, just constantly storing them at first in our memory bank. Then after habitual use, in the heart and then enters the subconscious. At this point in the subconscious, you do not have to think that hard about stealing, hurting, harming, yelling, rebellion, impatience, pride, lust, defiance, fear, and hatred to name a few. This is because through the course of one's life while filming on the set, they will more than likely encounter these "negative character weaknesses" at some point. Since everyone is different, the frequency at which one experiences these "negative character weaknesses" on a regular basis will vary. It takes a strong-willed person not to give into an environment that constantly embeds negative character weakness in your heart, which leads to the subconscious.

Do not think that just, because you were caught driving on a suspended license, have done a little time, and now it is all over. You see the problem with this situation really stemmed from when you are young and your brain first processed and realized that, when no one is around there is a good chance that you can get away with something. Then when we are confronted with what we have done, usually one of the first responses without thinking, because it is embedded in the subconscious is to use some "negative character weaknesses" as a defense mechanism. If some of these "negative character weaknesses" were dealt with at an early age maybe, the reason why the license was taken away in the first place would not have happened. If you are sincere about changing the way you make decisions then you must do a reality check on you. After you have made a list of "negative character weaknesses" and negative character weakness phrases, then describe all of those weaknesses to many other people but using someone else's name. This will give you an opportunity to see just how people really feel about you, without you telling them it is you. If your "negative character weaknesses" stem from youth, you must ask yourself; do these influence my thoughts to make an informed decision? If you can answer yes, then you have to ask yourself is this weakness necessary and does it really help promoting good decisions. If it is not, then make a daily effort to stop letting it influence your thoughts. Since the weakness was from youth up and deeply rooted, you must show progress by documenting how you handled each problem or situation that exposed that weakness. If you lived on an island paradise and one of your "negative character weaknesses" was anger, unless you ran into a situation or problem that exposed your anger you would not feel the need to work on it. You may not realize just how bad your problem was. Does constantly walking around "blowing up" at people and wondering why people are getting angry, (when you did not do anything) sound familiar? If you do not balance "negative character weaknesses" while in the heart, they usually enter the subconscious where they lay dormant until a person, problem, or situation exposes them. This will awaken them to begin mental combat with each other to see, which one will have the loudest voice to be unleashed. The one with the loudest voice is the one that works with another one, which is desire. Together they take the blame for the person choosing to act out on their thoughts. This is the answer to "why," when people are asked, "why" they did what they did or they say they do not know why.

CAST MEMBERS

Cast members are people that directly or indirectly influence your life. These are also people that you have direct contact with whether in conversation in person or by some other form of communication. A lot of the filming for the most part is in your thoughts and in your mind. Please understand that even though you may have done a good job working on your "negative character weaknesses", you still will make decisions that other people will not agree with.

Because everyone is different and does not work on their "negative character weaknesses" at the same time, you are going to encounter differences in opinion. To have disagreements is a part of life. Since you are the main character in your film, you cannot rely on cast members to do your job and take the lead actors spot when you should be doing it. You will be surprised to learn how many cast members are relying on you to step up to the plate and not only accept the leading role but lead by example so they can gain the confidence needed to become lead actors in their life film. You should view all problems from the standpoint of trying to fit a puzzle piece inside the puzzle. On the outside, the problem is apparently obvious, but with the problem comes the test, which pertains to the inside. The test in the inside is to see if you will work on your esoteric negative/ regular "negative character weaknesses" and balance your positive character traits.

Responding with a good response tends to attract positive vibes from cast members and in like manner, negative response tends to attract negative vibes from the cast members. When a cast member plays the part of working your nerves, you need to thank him for helping you work on your negative character weakness for free. In addition, tell him or her "The Creator knew I needed help with anger and you're doing a great job working my nerves for free." Thank you for you being you is what you need to tell the oblivious cast member that is still plugged into the old way of thinking. All they are doing is just playing their part in your movie and I am trying to enlighten your mind of the influence of "negative character weaknesses." You must approach the problem with the mindset that it is the cast member or problems job while on the set or on earth in your movie to do what it is doing, and it is your job to recognize what and when it is doing it. This is so that you can take advantage of working on your "negative character weaknesses" for free. If you refuse to work on your "negative character weaknesses" they will influence you and put limitations on how you deal with most people and problems.

You can also place your mind on simmer and slow cook the positive responses along with the fun mental release responses in your heart, so that it can feed your subconscious. While you are still on the set filming your life, work on your positive character traits with your family first and then to your neighbor, while you still have time. To make yourself feel good, make it a point to tell as many people as you can, that you appreciate them for them being them. Make sure you tell people up front that you would like to know and who you see on a regular basis, if they would help you work on your positive character traits, which is not complimenting people enough. Tell them to try to beat you saying you appreciate them first. This will enhance the feeling of excitement and elevate you and the person you complimented to "celebrity status" at the same time. If you are tired of making bad decisions that make you say, why am I or why do I still make bad choices, then it is time to change from the old way of thinking and try a new way. This book teaches you what to look for when problems or situations arise and how to cope with them long term. Most people are oblivious as to why they work other people's nerves. You have to realize it and then help them out by informing them about what they are doing. Also, help them realize the why and teach them how to recognize, and assess and process problems as they happen. If some people were aware of the limitations that are already subconsciously embedded in their hearts when we are confronted with situations, maybe they might do something different to receive a better outcome.

UTILIZING EXCUSES

There are people with legitimate hereditary mental disorders. However, people exasperate mental disorders through drug use and intensify them without balancing their "negative character weaknesses." They often elect to blame everything that went wrong in their lives on others or other circumstances; everything but their "negative character weaknesses" that they picked up throughout their life. For example: when the person first got on drugs, that situation exposed some "negative character weaknesses" that needed to be addressed (being a follower, desire, coveting, being gullible, wanting to fit in, lack of love or attention…to name a few). When I was a teenager, my peers tried to influence me by giving me tobacco. My father offered me marijuana. These influences failed because, although they used the drugs around me, I never possessed the negative character weakness of coveting what they had. The lack of wanting to be the lead character in your own life's movie and allowing other cast members to play the leading role is a sign that tells you, "I need help now." There are people that have stopped using drugs for years with much success. However, there are those that need more help. The people that are not strong enough to quit have to go back to the grass roots of the problem, which got them to try drugs in the first place.

The meaning of the word "esoteric" means: within, private, secret, confidential or hidden, and we tend to work on the obvious "negative character weaknesses." An easier way to know which "negative character weaknesses" are esoteric is to ask yourself: Which of my "negative character weaknesses" I would not freely admit to others? This will help you find your esoteric "negative character weaknesses."

The person that joined a gang has a similar problem. They allowed their esoteric "negative character weaknesses" to influence their thoughts, which limited their decision to only joining a gang. Sensitivity plays a major role in the makeup of a person's character. When a person sees you looking at them, gets angry, and says, "What are you looking at?" and wants to fight, he is really saying subliminally, "I am sensitive. Stop looking at me because it causes mental warfare in my mind." Sensitivity in males is taught as a bad thing in many environments.

Most of the time sensitivity is embedded in a male's mind from youth that it is a sign of weakness, which might set limitations on how well they might be able to defend themselves and their family. This is why most males will not admit that they are sensitive to things, which makes it an esoteric negative character weakness. Males do not realize that just because they suppress their sensitivity does not mean that you are not sensitive. This just means that you are expressing other "negative character weaknesses" not in place of sensitivity, but in front of sensitivity. Do not get me wrong there are cold, hard, callous people out there that really do not have any feelings or sensitivity. This is because their esoteric negative/regular "negative character weaknesses" were not addressed from childhood, creation, they are not human or they are partially human and the environment that was feeding their need to be negative was very influential. With many males, they can start out initially having a problem, person or situation expose their esoteric negative character weakness with sensitivity, which causes a chain reaction in the brain affecting the other regular negative character weakness like anger, frustration, bitterness, hatred, envy, and revenge. As these "negative character weaknesses" leave the heart they rest in the subconscious waiting to be awakened by the next excuse to allow them to be unleashed.

THE CIRCLE OF KARMA

I define the circle of karma as within the circle of life, you get out of it what you put into it. I was a victim of my circle of karma. I define my circle of karma as a circle with me at the bottom of it with a slight opening. Imagine the circle filled with 75% of hot water or negative energy and 25% of cold water or positive energy. My objective is to cool off with cold water or have a happy life making good positive choices rain down on me. The hot water represents all negative energy in my life, from thoughts and actions to any negative reality in my life. The cold water represents all positive energy in my life from thoughts and actions to any positive reality in my life. Because I chose to only, put in 25% positive energy to fight 75% negative energy, answers "why" my life took a wrong turn. This also answers some of "why" I am a victim of my own circumstance.

I was the first in line to renew my "mental membership" of un-forgiveness, anger, frustration, and revenge in my heart. I did this being very ignorant and oblivious to my self-imposed circle of karma. I did not take the time to realize "why" I placed limitations on myself. I allowed my "negative character weaknesses" to influence my thoughts to make bad decisions. The renewing of my membership also placed limitations on what a person has to say, how much I would entertain from what they have to say and just how happy I could be. The free will we have to choose to work on our "negative character weaknesses" is very important. Do not get to the point of no return by choosing to do wrong and think that things will work out, they will not.

I experienced a time in my twenties when a family member said something to me that upset me so bad that I left and went back to Germany, where I was stationed (cutting a thirty day leave early). I chose not to speak to my family for ten years. I had no idea that I had never forgiven my stepfather for how he mistreated me growing up. To make things worse, I called my stepfather and told him that I thought that the way he raised us was not right. The old buck sergeant told me that he did nothing wrong. That of course reignited mental combat in my mind that had been dormant. I was oblivious to the fact that negativity has a need to feed. This is why when I was on leave in Philly and a family member mentioned his name (or anything about him), mental combat engaged in my mind. I am sorry to this day for taking my "negative character weaknesses" out on my other family members (they had nothing to do with it). The comments my family member made did not justify not calling them for ten years. I thought that when I gave it to my higher power, I did not have to worry about it anymore. I was wrong. Every time I thought about him it would heat me up, because I had not purged my heart, which feeds the subconscious. I held a grudge and resentment for decades. My "negative character weaknesses" (grudges and resentment) placed limitations on my happiness with my family. This also affected how much I was willing to entertain what they had to say. I carried around a grudge and resentment in the backpack of my mind with other unaddressed esoteric negative/ regular "negative character weaknesses" and negative character phrases. I think that if my real father had never instilled in me that "you do not have to take nothing' from nobody," I would have still talked to my family for those ten years.

If a negative character phrase wins the "loudest voice battle in your mind", and you act on it, you can make decisions that you end up regretting. I had a paid four-year academic scholarship to Wilberforce University where I attended only one year and dropped out with a 3.7 grade point average. Even though school came easy to me, I allowed my "negative character weaknesses" to influence my thoughts and dropped out. My negative character weakness of pride with desire had the loudest voice. I told my mother, who flew out to Wilberforce, OH with me, that if they do not have my major (microbiology) we could get back on the plane and go home. When we arrived and I received my class schedule, it read "Biology Pre-med" as my major. My "negative character weaknesses" limited my positive responses to, "I will do a year", and that is what I stuck too. This was only after my mother begged me to do a year to see if I might like it. My mind was set on the path of being an immunologist and not a doctor. When you are a young, know-it-all, and choose not to listen to older and wiser people because of your negative character weakness, you can limit your level of education, which limits your job opportunities. In turn, this affects your happiness, because you cannot afford to live the kind of lifestyle you want to live due to limited job opportunities from a limited education. Now I do not allow people, problems or situations affect me long-term because I know "why." I try to help others recognize and get free of the "negative character weaknesses" that influence mental combat. I realized that since I cannot change other people, I could make changes in my character, which may inspire others to make changes in theirs.

I started to process and figured out that all esoteric "negative character weaknesses", regular negative character weakness, and negative character phrases placed limitations on me. I found myself limiting which positive responses I was willing to entertain to solve problems. I use the techniques I developed through the "Revelation of Why" to help process, observe and combat mental warfare on a daily basis. This starts by taking control of your life and not allowing limitations to order and/ or define it. Recognize what ignites your mental combat and advise the person or people in your environment accordingly. If they are not willing to stop triggering your mental combat, you might want to consider other options. This is suggested only if you feel the mental combat that you are experiencing may eventually take you to an extreme mental combat zone. If your situation does not drive you to the extreme mental combat zone, then consider "Forced Positivity."

FORCED POSITIVITY

This book teaches you how to apply "Forced Positivity," which means to force yourself to think positive most of the time and find the positive in the negative. This technique helps you to remove the stain in your brain of the old way of thinking. Performing these mental tasks in your mind, repeatedly over time, will begin the process of purging the heart of "negative character weaknesses," which feeds the subconscious. Appreciate today, while you still can because tomorrow is not promised. If you forget something or make a small mistake, do not speak negativity since it has a need to feed. If you have already spoken something negative, just say, "I mean," and compliment them or yourself. This will speak "Forced Positivity" into your life and attract positive vibes. Since positivity also has a need to feed, you must feed it, and then believe it so you can receive it!

RECEIVING CELEBRITY STATUS

One way to get negative thoughts off your mind is to receive "celebrity status" for little or nothing. "Celebrity status" is accomplished by telling as many as you know on a regular basis up-front that you are working on your positive character traits, which is not complimenting people enough, and could they help you with that. It will be a lot easier to start by asking the people that are in your sphere of influence or association, and then ask people that are in other environments (like your chiropractor, work, or where you live). People will more than likely agree with your endeavor, and you should thank them for their agreement. They may say, "For what?" and you say, "For being yourself." If you do not tell a person from the very beginning "why" you are doing what you are doing, when you tell them you appreciate (my unique form of appreciation – which is an exclamation of sincerity and has no pre-conditions) them, their response will most likely have a condition attached to it. For example, I complimented you because you are a nice person or because of what you did for someone today, whereas, a non-conditional compliment takes any potential stress off a person that makes a bad choice the next day. Thereby, they are truly appreciated, whether they perform to someone else's (or your own) expectations, or not.

When you tell a person, you appreciate them for them being them, you are initiating respect. Just like the old saying goes, "You have to give respect before you get it."

I believe we were created with a negative thought default. This just means that most of the time we humans tend to think negative without having to forcefully think that way. Some people may perceive giving a compliment without doing something to earn it is a sign of weakness or even insincerity. If those same people viewed the compliment as a way of showing respect instead of weakness, then they might be able to receive the compliment better. People who try to fool themselves into thinking that they do not need to be shown respect through a compliment do not understand some things about themselves. You see, a person may say, "I don't need you to compliment me." However, if they are in any position of authority the compliment that they "must" have been in the form of job performance. Owners, managers, and supervisors may not say they need to hear a verbal compliment; however, their subordinate workers under them "must" give them a compliment in the form of job performance. To many owners, managers, and supervisors a nonverbal form of compliment is better than a verbal compliment. Most of the time workers with very good job performance mixed with a good demand for your product or service will translate into more profits and someone else giving them a verbal compliment, whether it is from the public or other organizations etc. Having co-workers try to beat you saying, "I appreciate you" brings a little fun and excitement to most environments. If people in the corporate world experienced this, from the office executives on down to the lowest position, they would feel a little relief every time they leave their office and see someone different trying to beat them saying "I appreciate you." You will find that although you still have your workload that seems never ending, you feel good inside when someone tries to beat you saying "I appreciate you." With that smile on your face and laughter in your heart, that mountain of work you have to take on does not bother you as much. When you need a break from your workload, on your way to the bathroom find someone else that knows "why" you appreciate them and let them beat you saying it. This will help give you strength to go back and tackle that workload with joy in your heart. You will find that others will cheer you up without you having to spread your business around, if you are going through something. Of course, if your problem is serious seek professional help. The concept that I just mentioned can be applied in any work in environment, school, organization, club, and in public. I have used this same technique when I had things on my mind and did not want people to know what I was going through.

At some point, after continually using various compliments, you will find yourself competing to not only see who can be the first to compliment, but also whose compliment outweighs the other. Compliments should be sincere, first and foremost. Family and good friends will have a lot of fun trying this. Working on your "positive character traits" can be fun. Utilizing new compliments requires the mind to actively process positive thoughts, resulting in "Forced Positivity."

Performing these mental tasks in your mind over time, will begin the process of purging the heart of "negative character weaknesses," which feeds the subconscious.

POSITIVE RESPONSES TO "NEGATIVE CHARACTER WEAKNESSES"

These are positive responses to balance the negative character weaknesses that dwell within us. This is only a sample list. You can add to the list. You need to memorize at least two positive responses a day until you have remembered all of them.

1. Prayer
2. The circle of karma.
3. Returning a positive response to a negative insult.
4. 4. Instead of cursing, say "Got-down-off-my-horse" or "fiddlesticks".
5. Showing sympathy while you are mad instead of exposing the negative character weakness.
6. Accepting the fact that we cannot change cast members and uncontrollable problems that arise.
7. Asking the other person in a nice way to change the conversation if you know it is about to get heated.

8. Being honest telling the truth even when no one was around to witness what you done.

9. Not stealing while tempted.

10. Respecting another cast member (sleep, business property, how they do things, if they are moral).

11. Showing respect to others and in how you carry yourself.

12. Listen to music that you recorded to ease your mind of stress.

13. Understanding and gathering all facts before judging or making a decision on a situation.

14. Showing appreciation or thanking someone.

15. Manifesting calm and patience taking deep breathes turning the focus off the cast member or problem and recognizing your weakness and accepting the cast member or problem's role, which is to work on your weakness for free.

16. Resist running from a problem and figure out a way to make it work with either (understanding, concern, patience, love, or respect).

17. Purposely not limiting yourself to responding a certain way but allowing yourself to be open to a new perspective.

18. Increasing your faith when put to the ultimate test (loss of cast member).

19. Compromising on a decision that benefits both sides instead of just one.

20. Working on complimenting cast members for no reason. This lifts up one's self- esteem.
21. Apologizing for making a mistake.
22. Telling a cast member that you appreciate them.
23. Totally forgetting the conversation after an argument and choosing not to bring it up if it is not that important.
24. Giving a positive compliment that you notice up lifts a cast member.
25. In your mind envision an angel of the lord right next to you, either sitting down or standing up.
26. Resist the temptation to curse.
27. Resist the temptation yell and respond in a calm voice.
28. Resist the temptation to do drugs, by reminding yourself that the state your mind and body will be in when you are done will be worse than it is now.
29. Tell your subconscious that I control my body's desire, and not my bodies desire to control lustful thoughts.
30. I exercised control and restraint.
31. I refuse to let you get on my nerves.
32. I resist being gullible and overly trusting.
33. I fully process the problem before making a hasty decision.
34. I got advice from my parents before it made my final choice.
35. I was honest with my parents about_.

36. I accepted full responsibility for my decisions and actions without blaming someone else for my mistakes.
37. I refused to get angry today, or let you upset me.
38. I thought about what attracted me to you.
39. I thought about how you make me feel when we are together in love.
40. I took my mind off the problem we were having and focused on how beautiful you are.
41. Thank you for strengthening me in my area of because lord knows you are working my nerves good. (This is done with a smile on your face.)
42. I asked myself before I got on to you, if I was guilty of doing the same thing and since I was, I chose not to start and argument.
43. I chose not to use   against you even though you hurt me or made me mad.
44. I recognized which "negative character weaknesses" we are exposing and I balanced them.
45. I improved my positive character weaknesses.
46. I supported my mate today.
47. I supported my child today.
48. I supported my aunt today.
49. I supported my uncle today.
50. I supported a family member today.
51. I helped my family member today.
52. "Forced Positivity"
53. Not allowing your "negative character weaknesses" to be exposed.

"POSITIVE CHARACTER TRAITS LIST"

These are the traits that describe the positive nature of a person. These are traits that people should live by on a daily basis.

- faith
- healing
- love
- courage
- gentleness
- caring
- affection
- apologizing
- helping
- peace
- joy
- happiness
- passion
- concern
- trust
- will power
- drive
- determination
- complimenting
- compassion
- patience

Note: You can add more positive character traits

LIST OF COMPLIMENTS

These are compliments that should be used to encourage one another daily. Below is a list that you can add to.

1. Congratulations! – compliment for them being who they are.
2. "I appreciate you" – compliment for them being who they are.
3. Your amazing – to affect with great wonder.
4. Dazing – amazingly impressive, suggestive of the flashing of light.
5. Distinguished – (used of persons) standing above others in character, attainment, or reputation.
6. Outstanding – standing out among others of its kind.
7. Excellent – very good at the highest quality.
8. Fascinating – caused to be interested or curious.
9. Greatest – highest in quality.
10. Remarkable – notably or conspicuously unusual, extraordinary, remarkable.

11. Extraordinary – going beyond what is usual, regular, or established.

12. Sensational – producing or produce a startling effect, strong reaction.

13. Good – having desirable or positive qualities especially those suitable for a thing specified.

14. Terrific – very great or intense.

15. Tremendous – extraordinarily large or extend, amount, power, or degree.

16. Unparalleled – radically distinctive and without equal.

17. Astounding – bewildering or strikingly dumb with wonder.

18. Wonderful – extraordinarily good, used especially as intensifier.

19. Stupendous – great in size, force, or extent as to inspire awe.

20. Fantastic – extraordinarily good or great; used especially as intensifiers.

21. Exceptional – far beyond what is usual in magnitude.

22. Brilliant – surpassing excellence, having, or marked by unusual and impressive intelligence.

23. Beyond belief or understanding.

FUN MENTAL RELEASE RESPONSES

The purpose of this session is to show your creativity in compiling a list of Fun Mental Release Responses that allow you to blow off some steam at the person if you know them or to yourself in a fun way. All of these responses are delivered with a smile on your face. You must learn how to transfer all of the negative energy into positive energy. If what the person or thing that was, done to upset you is not that serious, then express your concern and then forget about it. If you hold on to it, it will control and consume your thoughts. Totally forgetting about the situation once both sides have had a chance to express their opinion and complimenting along with Fun Mental Release Responses is one of the best ways, I know how to move forward without having to carry the mental baggage with you. You can feel free to come up with your own. If replying with a smart remark is something you have done from a youth up, then ask yourself when you are experiencing problems, is this weakness really helping the problem or making it worse and is it influencing your decision. Most people that are smart with other people may say, "I don't care if you get smart back with me." However, let it be someone they do not know. You will find that most people that get smart with people cannot handle the same treatment done to them for no reason. If one of your weaknesses is being smart, when you first encounter a problem with a person acknowledge the problem and recognize your weakness. Then resist the temptation by replying with a compliment instead of a smart answer. Watch the other person will either show empathy, sympathy, or appreciation for your response. Of course, a callous person will not care. You should add your own response to reflect your personality in a loving way.

A few examples of Fun Mental Release Responses:

1. Boy, I bet you taught the class on how to stress a brother/sister out.

2. I bet you wish you could get paid for professionally working my nerves.

3. LORD knows I got problems with and you are doing a good job working my nerves.

4. I just want to thank you for the outstanding job you are doing working my nerves, helping me work on my "negative character weaknesses".

5. Does it ever frustrate you knowing you have the talent to work on my nerves so well and not get paid for it?

6.   I bet you gave your teacher a block of instruction on how to work his nerves, didn't you?

7.   I have to give it to you, you must have invested a lot of time and study at your job, because if I were paying you, I would have to promote you on how good a job you are doing…working my nerves!

8.   How does it feel working my nerves for free? Do you ever wonder just how much time it cuts into your productive life schedule?

9.   Shoot…let me find the joker that said that you got a –A in working my nerves at the University of Stressing Me Out.

10. I bet you get the same feeling that you get from sitting on tacks when you do not work my nerves.

11. I bet if you can work my nerves this hard without thinking about it, then becoming the President of Nerve Workers Union is a shoe-in.

12. What do you discuss at your nerve worker meetings anyway?

13. "So how many employees do you have?" He or she may say, "what employees?" or "what are you talking about?" You respond, "You know, the ones that walk around watching you work my nerves."

14. I saw the letter you got from Stressors' Anonymous asking you to renew your membership, looks like you re- upped for a lifetime membership.

15. Just say no to the organization of nerve workers.

16. I am sure you can go at least one hour without working my nerves.

17. Do you think you can be late at least once for your Nerve Workers can make a difference meeting?

THE ACCOUNTABILITY CHART

The purpose of this session is to learn how to assess and address your "negative character weaknesses" that influence your thoughts. The first thing is to get an understanding of how you feel on a regular basis. Are you normally a mad, sad, or upset person? Are you a happy go lucky person? Are you unfazed by people, things, or situations? The goal is to determine how you feel on a regular basis. Is the way you feel on a regular basis a normal behavior that most people would agree is a good way to feel or is it not a good way to feel? Try to take from your list some "negative character weaknesses" that best describe how you feel on a regular basis. Then recognize whether that character weakness is helping you or hurting you, and then do something about it whether good or bad. If it is a good trait, then improve it or if it is a negative character weakness reduce it or balance it. Then use the positive responses to deal with the "negative character weaknesses" you are experiencing on a daily basis.

This chapter describes how to fill out the accountability chart. This will serve as a gauge and a reminder of how far you are progressing. This resource can be used as a reminder of how to deal with similar situations. By documenting, you will have a daily testament of what you have done to improve your relationship. The goal of this session is to teach you how to keep track of your weaknesses on a daily basis and then add them up at the end of the week.

Maintaining documentation increases the ability for accountability of your actions. Documenting makes you more aware of where you stand with situations or problems. This also lets you know where you stand with your "negative character weaknesses" and positive traits. It would be a good idea to memorize the list of possible positive responses to the "negative character weaknesses" list. Make room at the bottom of the list to add your own possible positive responses as well. You must memorize at least two of your positive responses off your list every 2 days until you have all of your positive responses memorized. This can be done by writing down the two positive responses at any point of the day, every day. It is up to you to choose which "negative character weaknesses" to work on. In addition, it is a good idea to start on the ones that are triggered to a short fuse in the brain. You want to get to the point where none of the "negative character weaknesses" faze you and will not have any influence on your decision- making in the present or the future. Each person will be given 10 minutes to write down all the areas that they feel they are weak in as far as personality treats or "negative character weaknesses". Then each person will spend 10 minutes compiling the various list mentioned. You are shown how to do this while having fun at it. First, compile a master list of negative character weakness that you intend on working on. Either make a separate esoteric negative character weakness list or place the esoteric "negative character weaknesses" at the top of your regular "negative character weaknesses." Make a list of esoteric catalyst phrases. Then start taking about one or two weaknesses to work on from the master list.

You will work on one or two weaknesses every day for as long as you decide. As each situation or problem arises never, document the problem. Only write down which negative character weakness you are working on, the positive or negative points and the solution or the positive way you handled the situation from your positive response list to improve your character weakness. It is totally up to you if, you want to write down the problem at the moment in time. You will also write and keep a track of your positive character traits or trigger words that you work on daily. In addition, you will see which one of you is making progress or maintaining consistency. This way you can immediately see which character weakness you need more help with on a daily basis. Whenever people say, they need to make a change to the way they are doing things and begin the process, get the recognition you deserve. For example, if you say I am going to work on my short fuse, well every time you stop yourself from getting upset you should reward yourself with a point. Every time you return a positive response for a negative response, you should reward yourself with a point. What I am saying is you should reward yourself points for the things that you are already doing to make changes in your relationship and your life. You can then look back in the book and see where your character has progressed. You can also see areas where you regressed or went back to the same state of mind. If you are in a relationship and nothing is going fine, then you pick from your list of "negative character weaknesses". If you are in a relationship that you need healing, bonding, trust etc. then, after your mate makes his or her list, you both should agree to let each other pick the negative character weakness that will help you heal faster. I suggest that you try only one or two weaknesses at a time until you have gotten use to the book. Construct a chart for your weaknesses that has point values. There is a positive side and a negative side on the chart. The chart was specifically designed this way to help positive and negatively perceived thinking people get each other to meet half way or agree to work on weak areas without making the negatively perceived thinking person feel that they are a bad person just because they have a negative outlook on life and things in general. For example, a negative mate might want their positive mate to be more kinky or sexy. Although they are not challenging each other for this at the end of the week, the negatively perceived thinking person can suggest different things that are within reason for the positively perceived person to try.

Depending on the response of the positively perceived person they may have to utilize positive trigger words from their list to get points to help them handle the request. Every time the positively thinking person displays negative emotions, they get one point or as many as it takes until the positive trigger words have won the battle. That being said, the object is to build peace, love, trust and unity and balance. If a negative person is not allowed to express some of their emotions that they fear will upset the positively thinking person, then they may keep it bottled up, seek it somewhere else or try to work together with being released of it unless it is something that could just make the relationship better. For each weakness that you have worked on and responded in a positive manner give yourself 1 point and for any negative response subtract 1 point. You can only add points on the day that you are working on. For example, if you are working on Tuesday and you forget to write down all the points from your positive response list that day and now it is Wednesday; well, it is too late to add points to Tuesday while on another day. However, if you work difficult hours that require your day to switch over into the next day then conduct your schedule as you see fit that works best for you. Just base it off of a twenty-four-hour day. This way you are showing that you really want to win at the end of the week, because you are making an effort to make sure you can obtain the most points you can get without losing them the next day or twenty-four hours. After you pick the one or two negative character weakness to work on, you should try to pick at least two positive responses that you say to yourself or aloud to help you remember what to think of when your "negative character weaknesses" is exposed.

By constantly reviewing your list for the most positive responses you can think of when problems arise, you are starting the mental healing process of pouring positive thoughts in your mind. This over time with habitual use you may permeate the heart, which may influence the subconscious and allow you to have more pleasant thoughts without having to think about having pleasant thoughts. This mind set will help you deal with problems as they arise. On your chart, you must write a start time and an ending time of that day. If you work at night then you work out the best starting time and ending time. Really how much of the day you devote to working on your negative and positive character traits are totally up to you. Make up a challenge that you and all participants agree to. If you are doing this book with a mate or a friend, you can see who will end up with the most points at the end of the week and maybe take your mate or friend out to eat if that is what you agreed to. The one with the least number of points may have lost the contest that week; however, two winners emerge victorious a winner and a co-winner. The one with the most points win the challenge and the co-winner wins by participating in help-ing transform and balance a family member, lover, friend, or foes weaknesses into areas of strength, trust, and value for each other. This way you are working on your relationship whether mate or friend and turning it in a fun experience. If you do not have the funds, you can turn it into physical fitness fun. For example, if at the end of the week you had the least number of points, you can set between the two or three of you a workout schedule for the loser. If you cannot work out due to an injury or disability, you can agree to make the loser watch something that they would probably never watch on TV with you. You could agree that the loser takes you on a vacation. Competition usually brings out the best in us. Whatever you come up with, that will serve as an added motivation to do this book together while improving you and your relationship.

It is easy to convince yourself that you do not need to write down your character improvements, because you can see them in your daily walk. Just remember that we are human and you could be doing well for a long time, but as soon as you handle a couple problems negatively back-to-back all of a sudden, the exaggerative terms are used. You will hear phrases like you never, and you always.

If you are dealing with your mate, having a documented written account of your achievements can allow you and her to reflect on the positive and motivate you to be more motivated to prove that you can do it again. If it is a friend, you can show the friend your documented written account and use it to regain momentum to press forward and prove that you can do it again. This way you will have a written record that you can constantly refer back to, to dwell on in a positive way. Most importantly, you will have a record of the truth and not speculation going off what you thought you done and forgetting some other things that you have done. As time moves forward, our memory begins to fade and we do not recall many things in the past. Without the visualization of documentation and a verification system that documents the progress to combat a daily problem within us, we will forget. We will disregard or not care about a serious internal problem that needs addressing daily. It is not a good thing to dwell on the bad things in the past, but it is a great thing to reflect in a book your positive achievements on a personal level.

ACCEPTING DIFFERENT PEOPLE'S ROLE IN LIFE

Never allow jealousy to influence your thoughts over another cast member just because: He or she is your adversary or enemy, you see this can make you stronger and improve where you are weak. By having an enemy, your practice is put to the test. Maybe a co-worker got a promotion over you. Instead, learn from your experience and improve you so that in the future, if you try again or go somewhere else you will have a better chance at being promoted. This is if there is no chance for advancement where you are. He or she has better-looking women. Instead, improve yourself and get your mate to do this book with you so that outer beauty will not compare to the internal beauty that you both can possess within. He or she has a better car than you; instead improve yourself so that you can fix the things that you are lacking in your character like education, self-esteem, or a better job. You do not have a lot of money or fame. Instead, work on improving your weakness and motivate yourself to become that person with money and fame.

You must process that it is other people and problem's job as cast members to work on your "negative character weaknesses", and help you work on your positive traits for free. By doing so this satisfies the why people do what they do. You do not have to accept the why, but as long as you understand the why for yourself or the person or the problem you will have an easier time moving forward in society at a pace that is acceptable for you and society. Remember energy attracts energy. The more positive energy you exude the more will come back to you at some point.

Some people will never change and others will. As long as you understand this, you have done your part by working on your negative character weakness and improving your positive ones. You will not be limited in how you respond to problems and situations in life. Some hard- working cast members will try your patience, repeatedly, never realizing what they are doing. They are oblivious to the fact that they are compelled to strengthen you in whatever area is weakest in your "negative character weaknesses". They are a slave to their negative character weaknesses. You are the main character in your life, and everyone else is just a cast member. Focus on changing yourself and no other people or their problems. Try not to blame cast members for doing their job on the set in your show in life, which is to help improve your negative and positive traits, for free, unpaid. Remember, cast members are oblivious as to why/how they are building your character, for free, while serving as slaves to their weaknesses. Usually, you will find that once you tell a cast member that they are helping you work on your "negative character weaknesses" they will not like the sound of doing that *for free*. This does not apply to callous hearted people. It is a good thing that the cast members work on our character for free or we would be tempted to judge them on their performance.

Take advantage of problems when they arise so that you can also work on you for free. Try not to place limitations or obstacles in your own way, cast members do a great job of giving you enough of them already. Never limit yourself to thinking that I am just your average Joe or human being. In actuality, you have everything that you need to be successful already within you. You are waiting on you to give yourself a better role to play in this show or movie called life. Because you have the Free Will to decide how big of a role you want to play in life, use other cast members to help you succeed in the master role you want to play, whatever that role is. You are never too old to take on a leading role since you determine which role you want to play. Never say I am not smart enough or I cannot do it. Do not let your current situation set you back. Remember only you can change your role in your life. By balancing the "negative character weaknesses" and improving the positive ones, you remove all limitations in your life and can accept any role you want to play. Whatever role you want to play in your movie, obtain the knowledge necessary to play the part so, that you will be worthy of recognition. Remember cast members are real and you should do all that you can to learn from their production, so you can make improvements to your show. When you have had enough of watching other cast members take the leading role in your show you should motivate yourself to do whatever it takes to put yourself back in the leading role position whether male or female. Why is accepting the main character role so important in your life? If in the event that something happened to you, you would want one of your children to be strong enough to take the leading role, if no one else will. If family members life did end with the loss of your loved one you must accept your leading role, be strong and courageous, because other family cast members are counting on you. If you lead by example, your children would have a good mentor to follow.

It is up to you to accept the responsibility of the lead character in your life. By accepting the main character in your life, you make a choice to balance your negative character weakness allowing you to come out of bondage and refusing to utilize an excuse.

GROUPS THAT BENEFIT FROM THIS BOOK

This book would be beneficial for the school systems; because it will help, our youth begin their decisions to process instead of making decisions on impulse. Lately, the way in which you physically discipline your child is under heavy scrutiny, another approach is through this book using the "Revelation of Why." If children are our future, we cannot afford not to help teach them how to make better decisions. Why do children grow up and choose to do what they do? This has a lot to do with whether they had any help balancing their esoteric negative/ regular "negative character weaknesses." Schools should grade students on how well they handle correction, because how they handle correction affects how they interact with others. Those that are in authority should be able to come up with some kind of fair grading scale to assess, monitor, and grade how well students handle correction. When a student has a problem with correction, the esoteric negative character weakness is exposed and a chain reaction affecting the other regular "negative character weaknesses" ensues, which feeds the need to be negative. They then seek out other people and try to expose their negative character weaknesses, which triggers other esoteric "negative character weaknesses." When a person enters this phase, we usually see them acting out in retaliation for something that really had nothing to do with why they claimed they acted out in the first place. In many cases, a person will admit that they really do not know why they did what they did. This is because they chose to feed the need to be negative and the esoteric negative/regular negative character weakness that had the loudest voice influenced their thoughts to act out.

The initial esoteric negative character weakness that was exposed was correction, then anger, frustration, bitterness, and a host of others, which took the mind off the initial problem. Usually, desire and the negative character weakness that has the loudest voice (that wins the mental warfare in your mind) is to blame for you acting out on your thoughts. It is possible that desire can be the first negative character weakness to be exposed. One thing leads to another. This is why I believe a person does not have a clue about why they do what they do, because they do not take the time to observe, process, and fix the problem within them when the problem first presents itself. This mental process enters the subconscious after the "negative character weaknesses" have left the heart. I believe this is also why a person may say in their conscious mind (and out loud) that they really do not know why they chose to do what they did or responded the way they did, if they are not on any kind of mind-altering drug. This same scenario can be observed starting with any one of the esoteric negative/regular "negative character weaknesses" into adulthood and to some cast members making bad choices. There are some good examples of this in the chapters with skits. Holding a grudge resembles the same pattern, however many people are aware that they are holding a grudge and still elect to carry on with the same scenario as mentioned above.

To give you a more graphic visualization of esoteric negative/ regular "negative character weaknesses;" view them like old wounds that keep trying to develop a scab on them over time to heal. However, as various people, problems and situations present themselves; they re- expose some wounds reigniting the bleeding and pain, reinitiating the mental battle for who has the loudest voice. As the mental warfare goes on in the mind "negative character weaknesses" also compete with negative character phrases like; "I don't have to take nothing from nobody," "you cannot tell me what to do", "you can't teach me anything" and "I do what I want to do when I get ready." These wounds in the mind are part of the eight wounds mentioned earlier in this paragraph. Realize that although desire and the negative character weakness with the loudest voice may have won the battle, the war still goes on in the background with some waiting to be strengthened by the next person, problem, or situation. If we choose not to work on these negative weaknesses each day, we run the risk of re-opening old wounds in ourselves and others.

The tongue is an untamable thing capable of setting off mental warfare in others that you cannot imagine. This is because you never know what phase a person is in when you chose to "get smart" with them. It is a good practice to be polite to all people When time and age progress in a child's life, so does the esoteric negative/regular "negative character weaknesses" as well. Now as an adult, they are in a society where they are responsible for their choices, decisions, and actions. They walk around wondering why they made some of the decisions that they made and wishing they had put more thought into it. Even, if you put more thought into a decision, if the esoteric negative/ negative character weaknesses remain a part of your thought process, you may make a different choice, and still receive an unhappy result. Working on their positive character traits is vital to helping a child feel accepted and special. With children, you have to help them make esoteric negative/ regular negative character weakness list. They need help with making a negative character phrase list, a positive response list and an accountability chart and a compliment list.

I believe that this book would be very beneficial to inmates reentering into society. This teaches inmates how to interact with their family and how to balance their esoteric negative/ regular "negative character weaknesses", so they can make better choices in life. Obtaining knowledge from this book will help inmate and correctional staff relationship improve and minimize attacks on staff members. Working on improving their positive character traits allows them to take the focus off the issues that got them there and open up the door to a technique that promotes positive mental reinforcement. This book also shows them a way to work on changing them if they want to. The self-help book can be used while incarcerated.

Additionally, it can give them the necessary tools they need to not only show a change in them and their family, but to the community also. This book teaches them how to make an accountability chart, and a way to challenge each other to improve which could possibly be observed by staff, a negative character weakness list, a positive character traits list, a negative character phrase list, a response positive list, a fun mental release response list, an accountability chart, and a compliment list. This book would be great for all types of relationships for the same reasons mentioned above. Later in this book, you will be introduced to the way friends or mates can compete having fun while working on their character weaknesses. It is a fun new approach to dealing with problems. This book challenges your minds processes. It shows you how to take the focus off the problem and concentrate on yourself.

By applying the techniques in this book, you will be able to recognize "why" in a problem or situation as it happens and balance out the esoteric negative/ regular "negative character weaknesses;" and improve your positive traits. Also, by applying these techniques, you will know why you chose to react to whatever situation and be confident with your decision. Renew your mind from the old way of doing things and accept becoming enlightened in a new way to approach problems and situations without "negative character weaknesses" influencing your thoughts. If you would like to get a better idea of this book in the form of a visual perspective, then please purchase the workbook. Later in this book the skits will show you how the techniques are applied and the narrator will break down the mental warfare as it is happening in the characters mind. The skits will give you a mental and visual picture of possible origins behind these ticking time bombs walking around ready to go off at a moment's notice. I also have an Accountability Chart in the workbook that you write in to keep up with each negative character weakness you are working on to show your loved ones you are trying.

For more information, email Nate:
therevelationofwhy@gmail.com

SELF DIAGNOSES

The purpose of this session is to diagnose yourself. This is because although you can fool other people, you cannot fool yourself. You can try to deceive yourself into believing that you are something that you are not. However, this evaluation will help you soul-search the inner you and help you answer some important questions about you. The results that you are looking for in this session are to help you figure out you and why you are the way, you are. Once you see the real you on paper, what do you plan to do about it?

From your list of "negative character weaknesses" and negative character phrases ask yourself, the following questions as if you were diagnosing someone else you do not know:

1. Which of these character weaknesses is influencing my choices in relationships with lovers, friends, and people you meet?
   Example 1, 9,10,3,18,21,17
2. Which of these character weaknesses is holding me back from succeeding in life?
   Example

3.   Which of these character weaknesses is stopping me from being happy?

Example

4.   Which of these character weaknesses is stopping me from getting a mate?

Example

5.   Which of these character weaknesses is stopping me from being the main character in my movie called life?

Example

6.   Which of my "negative character weaknesses" influences me to fight in a negative way?

Example

7.   Which of my "negative character weaknesses" influences me to fight in a good way with motivation?

Example

Now you ask yourself these questions about you:

1.   Am I willing to do whatever, it takes to achieve; for example, question number 2 to succeed in life, question number 3 be happy etc.? Choose from the questions above. Example 1,2,3,5.

2.   Will I be satisfied with my life if I can achieve; for example, question number 4 having a mate, question number 5 being the main character in my life? Choose from the questions above. Examples 1, 2,3,4,5.

FINAL THOUGHTS

It is my intent to help bring families back together again only, if the parties involved are willing to sacrifice and work on their character weaknesses. I believe that we must show more respect toward one another because we never know what mental combat phase a person is in. With a little training and awareness, if we work together, we might be able to cut down the ticking time bombs walking around waiting to go off at a moment's notice to defend their thoughts. A lot of the knowledge in this book came from a revelation. Some of the experiences that I mentioned in this book are real life moments in time, while I was filming my life's story. I can recall one time while working at the Rutherford County Jail in Murfreesboro Tn., one of the most unexpected events happened. Because, at one time I tried out my technique going cell to cell on each of the male floors it paid off when a Sgt. called for available rovers to help lockdown a hostile inmate. I was working a post in medical which was totally on the other side of the building. Due to inmates in medical I had to wait until they were seen and escorted them back to their cells and then I proceeded to assist my coworkers deal with this hostile inmate. Keep in mind that months prior to this event I had went cell to cell asking the inmates if they would help me work on my negative character weaknesses. I said all you have to do is beat me saying, "I appreciate you" when I see you. Well, when I arrived at the D pod door, I observed my Sgt. with his back towards me about six feet behind the hostile inmate trying to talk him down. There were about seven deputies placed about six feet in front of the inmate in a semi-circle. When the top and bottom tiers realized that it was me trying to come in the pod it totally erupted. Before I could come in the door the inmates started yelling "I appreciate you, I appreciate you." As soon as the tower operator opened the pod door It was like entering a very loud coliseum back in the Roman days. The volume of the inmates was so loud that we had no choice but to stop giving all of our attention to the hostile inmate and go cell to cell calming down the pod. When the hostile inmate observed that we give our attention to calming down the pod he walked to his cell without any of us escorting him. It just so happens that we were over crowded at that time and the sheriff at that time shipped out two hundred and fifty inmates all around the state of Tennessee. I believe this event took place between the years of 2012 to 2015. I believe that it is safe to say that all personnel and inmates involved in that event will never forget what happened that day in the pod. Where one may deny what happened, I assure you that there are far more that will remember what happened due to the shear radiant display of power that was in the air. The was another time when I had a coworker who was very rude to me on channel one when I requested some inmates from his floor to medical. After I completed my medical traffic, I went up to the coworker's floor and said, "I appreciate you." I guess he thought that just because he was a lot bigger that I was he had some kind of advantage. So, he says to me "you appreciate me for what, bussing you out on the radio?" I said, "Lord knows, I needed help with working on my negative character weaknesses of getting angry at people and things and you just helped me out with that for free." Then I said, "how does it feel to work a full-time job and work over time working my nerves for free?" He said, "That's good, I never thought about it like that." Where did you get that from? I said, "I got it from the Revelation of Why. Then all of a sudden, this same deputy starts working with me for the next few days in a row. I said what is up with you working with me so many days? He said, "I want to learn some more about this Revelation of Why. The wisdom that I have gained in life has allowed me to listen attentively to people and safe guard my "negative character weaknesses" from being exposed, so that they will not influence my thoughts to make bad choices. I feel that to appreciate someone for him or her being whom he or she is and not for what was done for me, keeps me from holding a grudge or being mad at him or her when anger or frustration a rise in the future. It also keeps me safe from being accused of judging "What Is." My definition of What Is- it is the allowable perception of what man or creation perceives to be at that moment in time as long as it is in harmony with the powers that be whether good or bad, visible, or invisible. By exposing the mental warfare going on in people's minds at any given time you are better equipped to handle "What Is."

By doing this, my "negative character weaknesses" are being addressed on a daily basis. I utilize My creator, the technique I call "Forced Positivity" to make it through the dark and hard times in my life along with the circle of karma. I hope that you will join me in helping reunite and strengthen the family unit and our communities while reducing the ticking time bombs.

THE REVELATION
OF WHY WORKBOOK

This workbook will give people a comprehensive way to figure out the origin of why people do what they do in the skits. This also affords you the opportunity to observe the process and evaluate each skit and fill in the answers (in the blank) that you feel best describes what you read, and which esoteric negative/regular negative character weaknesses are used. Remember the mental thoughts revealed in this workbook only reflect the mindset of the characters in it. In the beginning of the workbook, you will have to make the following list: one of esoteric negative weaknesses, regular negative character weaknesses, negative character phrases, positive traits, positive responses, and a list of compliments, fun mental release responses, and finally, an accountability chart. As you go through each skit and figure out the best answers for the characters in each skit, you may find that if you apply some of the same answers you wrote down, they may help you in similar situations. Since all of the answers that are used will come from the various lists, it will be easier to relate to the characters in a personal way. You will learn to identify negative phrases that are causing mental warfare in your mind. You cannot stop them if you cannot identify them.

No one truly knows exactly what a person is thinking, but at least you can develop awareness toward the phase that a person may be in when you are talking with him/her.

After you make your list of negative character weaknesses, you can also view your list as if it is someone else and offer positive character responses to each esoteric negative/ regular negative character weakness. This is because we are usually able to offer some of the best advice to help others with the same problem before we use it. On a separate piece of paper, make a list of every environment that you see yourself in. Next, make a list that has all the new negative character weaknesses that you have adopted from each environment, carefully including the common negative character weaknesses that you have observed in all the environments. Finally, compare your original list to your own negative character weaknesses that you identified in all environments. This will help you influenced-search and determine which environment is feeding your "need to be negative". This will also help you figure out if total change is really an option in your life. This may seem like a lot, and it is going to take serious effort to change, but do it! You did not wake up the way you are overnight; it was a slow process over time. When you have completed this workbook, you will have a better understanding as to why people do what they do. You will have obtained a better awareness of the possible mental warfare that is going on in your kid's minds without having to ask them. Completing this workbook as a family will help build trust if all family members make an agreement not to hold anything against the other for being honest with their answers. Being honest with yourself, and your family, shows each family member who participates that you are sincere about changing your inner-self and purging your heart of negative character weaknesses. Remember, being deceptive and only writing down part of your negative character weaknesses only hurts you in the end. Even if you do not share this workbook with someone else, just looking at your answers and reminding yourself on a daily basis what you need help with will help reinforce change. These skits will give you an idea of how many people are living in denial and carrying around their negative character weaknesses into every environment, just waiting for you or someone else to expose what already lies dormant in their mind. There is an obvious anticipation for a person to allow problems or situations to expose what is already in them. This is because negativity has a need to feed. When you get to the skits below just remember that the answers are only a guide. Your real-life situations well dictate different results all depending on how you handle them and how you view them.

MAKE A LIST OF ESOTERIC NEGATIVE CHARACTER WEAKNESSES

1.
2.
3.
4.
5.
6.
7.
8.
9.
10.

MAKE A LIST OF REGULAR NEGATIVE CHARACTER WEAKNESSES

1.
2.
3.
4.
5.
6.
7.
8.
9.
10.

MAKE A LIST OF NEGATIVE CHARACTER PHRASES

1.

2.

3.

4.

5.

6.

7.

8.

9.

10.

MAKE A LIST OF POSITIVE TRAITS

1.

2.

3.

4.

5.

6.

7.

8.

9.

10.

MAKE A LIST OF POSITIVE RESPONSES

1.

2.

3.

4.

5.

6.

7.

8.

9.

10.

MAKE A LIST OF COMPLIMENTS

1.

2.

3.

4.

5.

6.

7.

8.

9.

10.

MAKE A LIST OF FUN MENTAL RELEASE RESPONSES

1.

2.

3.

4.

5.

6.

7.

8.

9.

***Start applying the knowledge that you have learned from this book and document them in the separate workbook available on line below. As you will see this will help the communication improve between as they say men being from Mars and women being from Venus:

SKITS FOR THE REVELATION OF WHY

SCENE ONE

Narrator: This skit will reveal some hidden things that are within us. These skits will challenge people to start to pay attention to how they come across. There are lasting effects that come from various environments. Some environments awaken our dormant esoteric negative character weaknesses, which influence our thoughts to make bad choices. This skit was also designed to have you be on the lookout for the why you have the need to feed the way you are and where it comes from when you're feeling negative. Please understand that this is only one potential scenario of many. Depending on the environment and association you are subject to enhance your negative character weaknesses without you even knowing it. The two main characters are Matt and Sam.

Matt comes from a poor family and Sam comes from a rich family. Matt and Sam are best friends. The first environment is in Matt's home. In this scene the man that plays the father Mr. Johnson tells the man playing the role of the son called Matt,

Mr. Johnson: I received a call from the school today telling me that you were starting trouble with other young men.

Narrator: He starts yelling at him asking him "

Mr. Johnson: What is wrong with you, why do you have to bully people?

Narrator: He does not respond for fear of hearing him yell even more.

Mr. Johnson: You are on restriction for a week.

Narrator: He tells him.

Mr. Johnson: This means no video games, computer, or hanging out with friends.

Narrator: Although he knows that he was wrong, the father does not know that his yelling exposed Matt's esoteric negative character weaknesses starting with the tone of his voice, correction, sensitivity, and resentment. His father thinks that just because Matt chose to be quiet to avoid hearing him yell more that he is giving him respect. What he is really doing is reinforcing and contributing to the mental warfare that is going on in Matt's mind on the esoteric level. In the young man's mind this same scene has been played out many times by his mother and father in other situations, like when he was very young and would ask for something 2 or 3 times. The response would usually have the same result, they would yell at him and tell him "I'm not going to tell you again or let me tell you again" in a hateful tone. Then threaten to punish him in some sort of way. Because the child back then could not get past the why he could not have what he wanted when he wanted it. This leads to him having problems moving forward in life and attracting negative energy.

Narrator: Because the child never could accept the why he could not have what they wanted when they wanted, the esoteric negative character weakness of resentment started to be embedded in the mind at a tender age. Since the child's mind is not fully developed, they cannot process the why they cannot have what they want when they want it. The delivery method the parent chose to message to the child was hostile and threatening to the child.

Narrator: There are many cases where even though the parent takes their time and explains the why thoroughly to the child, they still have a problem not accepting the why. This leads to the child acting out and listening to whichever negative character weaknesses at that time that has the loudest voice.

Narrator: Parents are usually oblivious as to just how and when they help start the mental warfare in their child's mind on the esoteric level. In Matt's case it is embedded in the heart and lay dormant in the subconscious until people, problems or situations expose it.

Narrator: Children grow up into adulthood very oblivious as to the mental warfare that exist in their mind competing for the loudest voice that influences their thoughts.

THE SECOND SCENE

Narrator: The second scene is a school environment. In this scene, Matt receives correction by one of his teachers. Matt is in the hallway talking to another student instead of going to class. The teacher tells him

Mr. Jacobs: You're already late for class.

Matt: I'm on my way.

Narrator: The teacher notices that he has not moved and tells him he will give his parents a call.

Matt: Mr. Jacobs, please don't call home; I'm already grounded for a weak. I don't need to get into any more trouble.

Narrator: Mr. Jacobs had no clue that Matt had just got in trouble and was on punishment for a week. Mr. Jacobs also did not know that Matt delayed going to class, because he had a need to feed is negativity. Matt's negative character weaknesses were starving for attention, which influenced his thoughts. This is why being on time for class was not a priority to Matt.

Narrator: Matt finally enters class and his teacher Ms. Reed tells Matt to go to the principal's office.

Mr. Climber: Why were you late for class?

Matt: I don't know why.

Mr. Climber: You better come up with a good reason why or I'll have to give your parents a call.

Matt: I promise it won't happen again.

Mr. Climber: If I find out that you are late again, I will not only call your parents, but you will have a couple days at home with your parents. This will help you realize why it's so important to be on time for class.

Narrator: Matt was in denial and was afraid to admit to Mr. Climber that his negative character weaknesses were in need to feed. This is why Matt was on a mission to find someone else and expose his negative character weaknesses to find relief. It is also true that Matt, Mr. Climber, Mr. Jacobs, and Ms. Reed are all very oblivious as to the mental warfare that exists in Matt's mind.

THE THIRD SCENE TAKES PLACE IN THE NEIGHBORHOOD

Narrator: Matt is walking home from school with a friend and he is taking his time to get there, because he knows he is grounded. Matt has an ongoing need to feed his negativity. Matt says to his friend, can you believe Mr. Climber jumped all over me and said he would call my parents because I was late for class.

Matt: What a jerk! You know how my parents are.

Narrator: As the negative character weaknesses begin to germinate, they are also shifting from one to another competing for the loudest voice to influence Matt's thoughts. Matt has now left his esoteric weakness phase and transitioned to his regular weakness phase (anger, rage, frustration, vengeance, short fuse, strife, corrupt mind, fault-finding, and boredom for that date with desire). As they walk home, Matt and Sam see a boy named Tim walking by himself.

Matt: Matt tells Sam, "Let's get him!

Sam: I don't know man; we might get into trouble.

Matt: "You don't tell me what to do; you do as I say and what I tell you to do."

Narrator: With the situation escalating, Matt continues getting angrier.

Matt: You see the way Tim looked at me? You know I got to do something now, because he looked at me the wrong way.

Narrator: At this point Matt has entered the negative weakness phrases, which are equally influencing his thoughts. Now one of Matt's negative character phrases kicks in his conscious mind influencing him to beat up Tim, since no one is around and he got away with this before in front of his friend. The thought of beating up Tim entered the conscious mind of Matt. Although Sam suffers from some of the same negative character weaknesses as Matt, the desire to beat someone up is not one that Sam shares with Matt. Just when hate won the date with desire.

Sam: Look I see someone coming let's get out of here. They both kept walking, acting like nothing happen since they were only in the planning stage and had not actually touched Tim. When Matt gets home Sam asks,

Sam: Why did you want to beat up Tim?

Matt: I don't know I was just bored.

Narrator: We see here that Matt's underlying problem starts on an esoteric level. He starts off not liking the tone of his father's voice yelling at him like in the past. Those esoteric weaknesses had a need to feed and awakened sensitivity and resentment. The regular character weakness invited themselves to the mental battle field. They were anger, frustration, and fault-finding tick for tact. Negative phrases were the last to enter the battle field. The prevailing negative character weaknesses that won the date with desire was hate. Matt was very oblivious to the fact that he had a need to feed his negativity. If Matt did not have his friend Sam with him at the time, he experienced mental combat the outcome could have been bad. This skit is a small illustration of one example of why a person may not end up knowing, why they wanted to do what they did. Once desire consumes the heart the mind tends to follow.

SKIT ONE QUESTIONS

FILL IN THE BLANKS OR MULTIPLE CHOICE

1. When Mr. Johnson starts yelling at Matt for bulling on other kids at school, which phase do you think Matt started out in esoteric or regular negative?

2. Which esoteric negative/ regular negative character weaknesses do you think are battling in Matt's mind while he receives a verbal tongue-lashing?

3. Which one of the esoteric negative weaknesses do you feel would win the battle in your mind? You can take from your list as well.

4. What would be the best response for you if you were Matt?

5. Which negative character weaknesses do you think revealed themselves in the teacher Mr. Jacobs when

he saw that Matt was not going to class after replying to him sure thing?

6. Which negative character weaknesses do you think were battling in Matt's mind when Mr. Jacobs told Matt that he would call his parents?

7. Which positive response from your list do you feel would have been appropriate?

8. Which negative character weaknesses do you feel revealed themselves when Matt being late interrupted Ms. Reed's class?

9. When Matt went to the principal's office list as many negative character weaknesses you can think of that were battling to see who has the loudest voice in Matt's mind.

10. Which negative character weaknesses do you think revealed them in Mr. Climber's mind when he asked Matt to explain why he could not be on time for class?

11. What would have been a good response to use when Mr. Climber asked Matt to explain why he could not be on time for class?

12. Why do you think Matt could not wait for school to be over?

13. When Matt sees Tim, which negative character weaknesses do you think were battling in Matt's mind?

14. Which negative character phrases do you think entered Matt's head when Sam said we should not do it because someone might see us?

15. When Matt told Sam the negative phrases, which negative character weaknesses do you think were battling in Sam's mind? These will come from your list and not the skit.

16. What was the original cause for Matt to come up with excuses for wanting to beat up Tim?

17. Which negative character phrase kicked in Matt's mind when he thinks in his conscious mind to beat up Tim? Pick from your list.

18. IF you were in Sam's position, would you have been strong enough to use a positive response to give Matt? Yes or no.

19. If you answered yes, then which one of your positive responses would you have used?

SKITS FOR THE REVELATION OF WHY

Scene Two

Narrator: The scene starts out at Matt's home while Sam is waiting for Mr. Thorp to arrive to help his friend and their family the same way he helped his family. This skit was designed to give you some ideas that you can use, if you want to change yourself. This skit also was designed to show you how to apply the techniques used in the book the Revelation of Why. It gives you a better understanding of how the techniques are applied.

Sam: I invited a man over to your house.

Mrs. Johnson: Sam why would you invite a stranger over to my house?

Sam: I thought he could do the same thing he done for my family for yours.

Narrator: The man that Sam was talking about the Revelation of Why knocks on the door and Sam answers it.

Sam: Hello Mr. Thorp how you doing?

Mr. Thorp: I'm fine thank you.

Sam: Come in and I'll introduce you.

Sam: Mr. Thorp this is Mr. and Mrs. Johnson and this is my best friend Matt.

Mr. Thorp: "How are you? It's a pleasure to meet you."

Mr. Thorp: Sam invited me here today, because he wanted your family to experience the same joy that his family is experiencing.

Mr. Thorp: I appreciate you with a smile on his face.

Mr. Johnson: I appreciate you.

Mrs. Johnson: I appreciate you.

Matt: I appreciate you.

Sam: I appreciate you.

Mr. Thorp: Can you explain to me each one of you, why you told me you that you appreciate me."

Mr. Johnson: I appreciate you for taking the time out of your schedule to come over here and show you're concern for us."

Mrs. Johnson: I appreciate you for having a concern to help families.

Matt: I appreciate you for doing something positive with yourself.

Mr. Thorp: I thank you, but I appreciate you for your being you, not for what you did or what you're going to do; today you might make me happy, tomorrow you might not, I just appreciate you for you being you.

Mr. Thorp: ''is anything wrong with that?''

Mr. Johnson: No

Mrs. Johnson: No

Matt: No

Sam: No

Mr. Thorp: Just so you understand, I do not appreciate the negative behavior from bad choices people make. Instead, I learn from other negative behavior to see how I can avoid falling into the same trap.

Mr. Thorp: One of the best ways I know to cheer up your spirits is to tell everyone that you know up front that you are working on your positive character traits and would they help you with that?

Mr. Thorp: Most people will be willing to help you work on you.

Mr. Thorp: Just tell the other people that all I'm asking in return is to beat me telling you that I appreciate you before you tell me, that way the anticipation builds and it's fun.

Mr. Thorp: You can tell that person that we will both receive instant celebrity status at the same time.

Mr. Thorp: If you and the person you are with are having a disagreement and all of a sudden that other person notices you getting most of the attention by someone letting you know how well they appreciate you, that disagreement will take a back seat.

Mr. Thorp: This is because that person is going to want to know how you know this person. You can tell the person I do not know that person; however, they know where I got it from.

Mr. Thorp: Let me show you something on my large pad.

Mr. Thorp: These here are esoteric negative character weaknesses.

Mr. Thorp: I believe that a lot of why we end up doing what we do originates with either these esoteric negative/ regular negative character weaknesses or negative character phrases.

Narrator: While he is saying this, he is turning the page displaying a list of regular negative character weaknesses.

Mr. Thorp: You may ask yourself why he is showing us this; this is because I'm trying to spread awareness about the origin from where what influences our thoughts comes from. And to show you a way to combat some of the ticking time bombs walking around ready to go off.

Mr. Thorp: I'm speaking of the mental warfare that goes on in our mind.

Mr. Thorp: When we have a need to feed our negative character weaknesses our mind battles to see who has the loudest voice to influence our thoughts."

Narrator: Mr. Thorp gives an example about a young man that gets into trouble for bullying other kids. The example resonates with the family. This scenario is the same one that Matt and his family just went through. As he is explaining Matt interrupts.

Mr. Thorp: Have you been talking to Sam?"

Mr. Thorp: No why?

Matt: This story sounds very familiar.

Sam: I promise you I never said a word about you or your family.

Mr. Thorp: Do not be alarmed, I have addressed many cases; I just chose this one out of many.

Mr. Thorp: I teach people to make a list of esoteric negative character weaknesses, regular negative character weaknesses, negative character phrases, positive traits, positive responses list, fun mental release response list and an accountability chart.

Narrator: While Mr. Thorp is mentioning these lists, he is displaying each one as an example.

Mr. Thorp: You must use a positive response every time you experience a person, problem or situation that causes you to think of negative thoughts.

Mr. Thorp: Which brings us to the definition of the Revelation of Why?

Mr. Thorp: The Revelation of Why is the process by which you make a conscious effort on a daily basis all day long, not so much to focus on the people or problems, but on your inner self at the time your thoughts begin to experience negativity.

Narrator: Mr. Thorp goes back to the chart and points at the esoteric negative character weaknesses and says,

Mr. Thorp: When we are very young, we develop esoteric negative character weakness, which means private or hidden.

Mr. Thorp: Many people still have trouble getting past the why they were treated a certain way.

Mr. Thorp: Why other people cannot conform to another way of thinking which causes mental combat.

Narrator: Mr. Thorp points to each esoteric example going down the line on his large pad.

Mr. Thorp: A person may have started out with being corrected by being yelled at for something as small as taking a cookie on the kitchen table.

Mr. Thorp: The problem is how the child was corrected in the child's mind.

Mr. Thorp: All the child knows is that he saw his older sibling get away with taking a cookie and nothing happen to him.

As soon as he takes a cookie he gets yelled at since the parent catches him in the act.

Mr. Thorp: Some children choose not to get into a yelling match with their parents. Other children choose to yell back.

Mr. Thorp: Some parents think that just because their child is quiet taking the tongue lashing that they are being respectful. One of many possible realities is the child is building up resentment for how they are being corrected.

Mr. Thorp: The mental warfare begins in Matt's mind starts with correction, the tone of the voice, sensitivity and then resentment.

Mr. Thorp: Negativity has a need to feed in order for it to survive.

Narrator: Mr. Thorp turns the page.

Mr. Thorp: The negativity leaves the esoteric phase and enters the regular negative character weakness phase.

Mr. Thorp: This is when the person experiences anger, wrath, rage, impatience, and a host of other negative character weaknesses.

Narrator: Mr. Thorp turns the page.

Mr. Thorp: The need to feed does not stop there, it conducts mental combat with negative phrases like; I don't have to take nothing from nobody, you don't tell me what to do.

Mr. Johnson: You don't tell me how to raise my kids.!

Mrs. Johnson: Just who do you think you are trying to tell us how to raise our kids?

Mr. Thorp: All I'm trying to do is help educate people who may not realize how they are contributing to the ticking time bombs that are walking around.

Mr. Johnson: We're not contributing to that problem, because our son might be bad, but he is respectful.

Mr. Thorp: A lot of parents are oblivious as to how their child truly feels about them.

Mr. Thorp: If you don't believe me, please allow your son to speak freely to express how he honestly feels about the things we talked about.

Mr. Thorp: Because this is for educational purposes, please do not hold his honesty against him.

Mr. Thorp: By you willing to open up and receive correction from your son you may not only learn from him, but you can start to build trust in your family unit.

Mr. Johnson: Matt is any of what this man is saying true.

Matt: I can't believe it.

Mrs. Johnson: What son, what's wrong?

Matt: All of what Mr. Thorp explained I have experienced at one time or another even about the cookie.

Matt: Even though I don't have any siblings, I got caught taking a cookie from my aunt Matte's kitchen table when I was very young.

Matt: My aunt saw my cousin take a cookie and yelled at me when I got one without asking.

Matt: Although I was wrong for taking the cookie without asking for it, my cousin was equally wrong as well and he didn't get yelled at.

Matt: Because I felt that my aunt was unfair and did not explain why she let her son have a cookie and not me, I started to develop resentment in my heart.

Matt: I was quiet when she yelled at me, but it led to resentment building in my heart and need to feed my negativity.

Matt: Later when we got home and my parents corrected me for something, I resented them.

Matt: I guess I had a need to feed my negativity as you say.

Mrs. Johnson: Matt, you sure this resentment didn't start with us and how we discipline you?

Mr. Thorp: Mrs. Johnson, if I may interject here, while we have Matt talking, we do not want him to shut down when he is pouring out his heart to you.

Mr. Thorp: When you start to question him like that, automatically in his mind he will set limits on what he will listen to and then tune you out.

Mr. Thorp: This is how the communication breakdown starts out.

Mr. Thorp: If Matt perceives that you are trying to be negative, he will be negative also, remember negativity has a need to feed.

Mr. Thorp: Remember Matt admitted that when he was corrected by his aunt, he was quiet. He will resent you in the same way, if you start badgering him.

Mr. Thorp: Matt will through his resentment along with the other negative character weaknesses and phrases into his mental back pack and continue to seek out others to expose their negative character weakness.

Mr. Thorp: Before you know it, Matt's acting out being influenced by the negative character weaknesses that have the loudest voice in his mind.

Mr. Thorp: I believe desire and the negative character weakness with the loudest voice shares the blame for why a person acts out or does what he or she does.

Mr. Thorp: For example: If Matt beat up someone and you asked Matt why he did it, he might say that he was just bored when the real cause came from his need to feed his negativity.

Matt: I can relate to that because it happened to me.

Matt: Even though Sam asked me why I wanted to beat up Tim and I told him I was bored; I really didn't know why I wanted to beat him up.

Mr. Thorp: This is because as your thoughts host the war in the esoteric phase and enters the regular negative character weakness phase you forget about the old war and focus on the new one at hand.

Mrs. Johnson: Ok now that we know where negative character weaknesses come from; why is it so important that I know about my son Matt's negative character weaknesses?

Mr. Thorp: It's important for you to know because later in life when you call yourself reaching out to help your son or form a stronger bond, he will still hold resentment for how you treated him.

Mrs. Johnson: Matt is this true?

Matt: Do I really have to answer that question?

Mrs. Johnson: Matt, you can tell me the truth baby.

Matt: Mom with all due respect, you, and dad yell at me so much; you make me feel uncomfortable talking to you about anything.

Mr. Johnson: Mr. Thorp what do you suggest we do?

Mr. Thorp: I suggest you work on your negative character weaknesses as a family.

Mr. Thorp: Start off telling each other you appreciate each other every day.

Mr. Thorp: Create the various lists that I showed you earlier and create an accountability chart.

Mr. Thorp: make an agreement that whoever has the least number of points accumulated has to do what is agreed upon. Everybody wins because you are all witnesses to participating in helping reestablish love, trust, and faith in each other.

Narrator: Mr. Thorp shows them the accountability chart.

Mr. Thorp: For each positive response that you use you get one corresponding point.

Narrator: Mr. Thorp gives them an example on his large pad.

Mr. Thorp: You must make a list of esoteric negative/ regular negative character weaknesses and a negative character phrases list.

Mr. Thorp: You must make a list of all the negative character weaknesses in all your environments.

Mr. Thorp: You must make a list of negative character weaknesses that you adopted in those environments.

Mr. Thorp: From the list that you adopted negative character weaknesses compare that with your original list of negative character weaknesses. Then find out which environments is feeding your need to be negative or the way you are.

Mr. Thorp: You must create a positive response list and a positive traits list or positive trigger words.

Mr. Thorp: You must create a fun mental response release list.

Mr. Thorp: Make an accountability list or purchase the book called The Revelation of Why.

Mr. Thorp: There is a positive and a negative side to the accountability chart.

Mr. Thorp: The chart was specially designed to help positive and negative thinking people challenge each other and communicate better and build trust love and unity.

Mr. Thorp: To get the opposite thinking person to do what you want within reason you can create a challenge or incorporate your bonding together.

Mr. Thorp: For example, a negative thinking mate might say, although we are not challenging each other to show more affection I want you to meet me half way and start showing more affection.

Mr. Thorp: On the positive side of the chart the positive person will have to document which positive trigger words that they can think of and get points if they struggle with being affectionate.

Mr. Thorp: If they handled the response in a negative fashion then they must give themselves a negative point. **Mr. Thorpe:** The same applies for both sides.

Mr. Thorp: The thing is trying to get the meeting of the minds, emotions, and personalities to meet half way or whichever, side will bring peace love and trust in the relationship whether platonic or intimate.

Mr. Thorp: It's a shame that there are people that really believe that getting the best education, best job and making the most money is all you need to do in life to be happy.

Mr. Thorp: When in reality you could be doing all those things and still be unfulfilled, miserable, sad, and wondering why.

Mr. Thorp: You should not blame someone else for all the limitations you placed on how you interact with people, problems, and situation in your life's story.

Mr. Thorp: When you choose to get smart with people and not respect their feelings, you are helping create or sustain resentment in them. And you are adding to the ticking time bombs out in the world that one day may go off on you for no reason.

Mr. Thorp: Just remember it's going to take a lot to get to the bottom of why you still are the way you are, if you want to change.

Mr. Thorp: Change is never easy, if you have mastered the way you have been doing things all your life.

Mr. Thorp: It's been a pleasure speaking with you, but now I must go to another appointment.

Narrator: The family thanks Mr. Thorp for coming over and Mr. Thorp leaves the house.

Sam: What do you think about what Mr. Thorp said?

Mr. Johnson: It sounds good, but that's a lot of lists to write.

Sam: I know, but if you don't do it along with other people in the world; you will be part of the problem contributing to the ticking time bombs.

Mr. Johnson: Matt are you a ticking time bomb waiting to go off?

Matt: No sir.

Mr. Johnson: Sam Mr. Thorp was wrong about what he said.

Sam: Well, it seems to be working for me and my family. **Sam**: Now I feel better about talking to my mother and father about what's going on with me instead of them making me feel like I'm less than a person and they don't have time for me.

Sam: Since I have a better understanding of the why I do what I do and why my parents do what they do; I have an easier time dealing with issues as they arise.

Sam: Now this doesn't mean that I agree with what they do, but since I have an understanding of the why, it's much easier accepting it and moving forward.

Sam: As problems or situations arise, I don't focus on the problem, but instead I ask myself which negative character weakness is being exposed.

Sam: This way I can eliminate the potential mental combat and enjoy my day.

Sam: The list of positive character responses and fun mental release responses really helps me not only handle problems, but it helps me work through it. Kind of like saying positive affirmations.

Sam: It's actually fun, because my whole family is competing to see who can get the most points.

Sam: Now we have something to celebrate every week together.

Sam: The best thing about this is even if I loss I still win, because myself and my parents are working on ourselves individually and keeping a log of it.

Sam: By looking at mom and dad's chart I have a more open mind as to why they respond and interact the way they do.

Sam: The chart and the list help them get a feel for what I'm thinking.

Sam: By looking at my list of positive responses they are better equipped to encourage me the way I need to be encouraged.

Sam: This list tells me that they are making an effort to change the way things have been going on and opens up the door to work on positive character traits like trust.

Mr. Johnson: That's good for you and your family, I got to go to work now.

Mr. Johnson: Bye everybody, I got to go.

SCENE THREE

Narrator: The next environment is a scene where Mr. Johnson is at work.

Narrator: Mr. Johnson sees a coworker and tells him, hi Fred.

Fred: I appreciate you.

Mr. Johnson: for what?

Fred: For you being you, not for what you did or what you are going to do.

Mr. Johnson: Have you been listening to a man named Mr. Thorp?

Fred: Nope, but I got a hold of a book that changed my family's life.

Fred: I just could not understand why when I try to reach out and help my son, he would just abuse me and have no remorse.

Fred: This book opened up my eyes to why he treated me so bad, after I helped him get out of jail and get him a place to stay.

Fred: It also taught me and him how to move forward in our relationship.

Fred: To take a closer look at how I was raising my son. **Fred**: I thought I was right following my parents yelling after my kids when they would do wrong.

Fred: Because my son was quiet and respectful when I yelled at him, I thought everything was fine.

Fred: It took me decades later and this book to realize that not only was my son treating me bad, but he had a need to feed his negativity.

Fred: The book explained, because of his need to feed his negativity and him not knowing the why he was treating others the same, he gave into the mental warfare going on in his mind.

Mr. Johnson: Thanks, my friend.

Scene Four

Narrator: The scene changes from work to back at home where Mrs. Johnson gets some company that comes over. Sam's mother Mrs. Pattie Ringer comes over to talk with Matt's mother Renee Johnson. Mrs. Ringer is at the door and says,

Mrs. Ringer: Hi Renee, I just wanted to say, how you are doing and I appreciate you.

Mrs. Johnson: I appreciate you?

Mrs. Ringer: What do you appreciate me for?

Mrs. Johnson: I appreciate you for being one of the nicest women I know.

Mrs. Ringer: I thank you, but I appreciate you for you being you, not for what you did or what you're going to do.

Mrs. Ringer: Mr. Thorp taught us from a book that there's nothing wrong with telling someone you appreciate them for the reason you mentioned, but usually there is a condition behind it when someone tells you they appreciate you.

Mrs. Ringer: The kind of appreciation that Mr. Thorp spoke off without conditions made me feel a little better. We all make mistakes constantly.

Mrs. Ringer: That being said, I do not condone people making bad choices that cause harm to people.

Mrs. Johnson: I never thought about it like that.

Mrs. Ringer: Even in a totally negative environment respect and appreciation must be given without question.

Mrs. Ringer: The respect and appreciation may not be obviously shown; however, it must be there.

Mrs. Ringer: When major companies hire employees, they must perform to a certain level of expectation.

Mrs. Ringer: Owner, Supervisors and Managers may not want you to compliment them out loud.

Mrs. Ringer: They already know that if the employee performs and exceeds their expectations, they will receive compliments from the public, media, higher demand for product and other sources.

Mrs. Ringer: Have you guys had a chance to talk with Mr. Thorp yet?

Mrs. Johnson: He actually just left not too long ago.

Mrs. Ringer: If you have some time, I just wanted to share with you how Mr. Thorp has changed our life.

Mrs. Ringer: We thought that pressuring our son into being what we wanted would make him and us happy, but all it did is build up a mental wall of concealed resentment.

Mrs. Ringer: Renee, I know that you're a strong woman, but please don't make the same mistake we were making with our son with yours.

Mrs. Johnson: If it was anybody else telling me this you know; I would let them know with the quickness that you don't tell me how to raise my child.

Mrs. Johnson: So, what are you suggesting?

Mrs. Ringer: Now that Mr. Thorp has shown us how to approach our son through this program, we have used it to greatly improve our whole family relationship.

Mrs. Ringer: See if your son and your husband will try this program with you.

Mrs. Ringer: You do not have to ask Matt to admit to what's wrong with him; you will see it on his list of negative character weaknesses that he is working on. **Mrs. Ringer:** Only encourage one another as you encounter various problems and situations to choose as many positive responses as you can.

Mrs. Ringer: This will begin to purge out the negative character weakness embedded in the heart which enters the subconscious.

Mrs. Ringer: The best thing whether you win or lose when you are competing for points in the program is that you are all growing towards change in your family and in life and minimizing the potential ticking time bombs in the world.

Mrs. Johnson: I thank you for being a true friend and sharing that with me.

Mrs. Ringer: You're Welcome, well Renee, I have to run some errands and I'll talk to you later.

Mrs. Johnson: Bye and thanks again for coming by.

Scene Five

Narrator: This next environment displays a scene with Matt and Sam walking home to Matt's house and they meet some friends in the neighborhood.

Sam: Hi guys what's up?

Matt: What's up?

Narrator: They all wave and say hi, as they get closer to one another.

Sam: I appreciate you, Scott.

Scott: For what smarting off to my mom?

Narrator: Sam had no idea that Scott was in need to feed his negative character weakness. Scott had just shared with his friends about how he got smart with his mom and then shared it with Sam and Matt.

Sam: No for you being you, not for what you did or what you're going to do.

Scott: Thanks man that's the best encouragement I've received in a long time.

Sam: A man named Mr. Thorp changed our whole family's life for the better.

Scott: Oh yeah.

Sam: A man named Mr. Thorp came over and told us about the Revelation of Why.

Sam: Would you like to know the core reason as to why your mother or father yells at you when they don't like what you are doing.

Sam: I bet you think that the only reason why your parents yell at you is because they are just continuing to pass on how they were raised as a child.

Sam: That's only part of the problem; the rest goes back to what Mr. Thorp called esoteric negative/ negative character weaknesses.

Sam: Mr. Thorp taught us that if negative character weaknesses are never addressed or balanced on a daily basis, they lay dormant in your subconscious waiting for a person, problem, or situation to awaken or expose them.

Sam: I bet you're like me, since I had a hard time accepting correction at a young age, me not knowing it; it led to the mental warfare that goes on in my mind.

Sam: You probably were like me starting in the esoteric phase struggling with correction which placed limitations on what your mom had to say,

Sam: Esoteric meaning something that is private, hidden, or confidential

Sam: Your mind limited how long you were going to entertain what she had to say and how you were going to respond to how she talked to you.

Sam: Then you went from the tone of your parent's voice, to sensitivity to resentment still within the esoteric phase.

Scott: Yes, I did.

Sam: As the battle to see who has the loudest voice continues in your mind, you enter the regular negative character weakness phase exposing your anger, bitterness, wrath, and vengeance.

Scott: How do you know so much about me when you don't live with me?

Sam: Then the loudest voice with desire gets the blame for you acting out on your negative character weaknesses.

Sam: I bet you told as many friends as you could.

Scott: I did, but how do you know?

Sam: Mr. Thorp taught us in the book that negativity has a need to feed and it will find an environment to feed in.

Scott: How does Mr. Thorp say to stop this problem?

Sam: He tells us to first make an esoteric negative/ regular negative character weakness list, negative character phrase list, and a positive character traits list for every negative character weakness, a fun mental response list and an accountability chart to keep up with your progress.

Sam: If you want to soul search you must make a list of negative character weakness in every environment.

Sam: A list of which negative character weaknesses you adopted from those environments.

Sam: Lists of all the common negative character weaknesses from your list and then say to you are these negative character weaknesses helping.

Sam: Are they placing limitations on me in any way, stopping me from being what or who I was meant to be in life.

Sam: I know this sound like a lot, but this brought my family back together and we're having a lot of fun with it.

Narrator: Matt and Sam's family learned The Revelation of Why and how to apply it in an everyday setting.

Narrator: Sam was able to appreciate the techniques from The Revelation of Why first by using it with his own family.

Narrator: After receiving positive results he decided to inform his friends. Matt learned a valuable lesson about why he does what he does without thinking about it.

Narrator: Sam and Matt's parents were taught a way to communicate with their kids in a way that works on building love and trust.

Narrator: Please understand that it is important to note that you should not condone bad behavior in the form of an appreciation.

Narrator: Telling people, you appreciate them in a negative environment sometimes can improve it. The overall atmosphere can improve greatly.

Narrator: The atmosphere in offices could possibly improve, if employees took the time to tell each other I appreciate you for you being you, not for what you did or going to do.

Narrator: I believe that people respond differently to a person that knows the why I appreciate them from the one with a condition.

Narrator: Please understand that there is nothing wrong with letting people know, why you appreciate them in the normal sense with a condition attached to it.

QUESTIONS

1. When Sam starts to tell Matt about how his family life improved, which limitations did Matt place on Sam?

2. Mr. Thorp says, I appreciate you for what?

3. What is the major difference between Mr. Thorp saying I appreciate you and the whole family saying I appreciate you?

4. Where does Mr. Thorp believe the origin for why people do what they do comes from?

5. What awareness is Mr. Thorp trying to spread?

6. When we experience difficult people, problems or situation what goes on in the mind?

7. Which negative character weaknesses do you think went to battle when Mr. Thorp started to tell his story about a young man bulling other kids?

8. What does Mr. Thorp say every time a person, problem or situation entices you to think negative?

9. What is the definition of the Revelation of Why?

10. What does esoteric mean?

11. Write down in your own words why when a person was young, he or she could not get past the why they were corrected, which lead to them carrying this open wound in their mind?

12. In your own words write down some ways that you feel that you have held on to resentment. You can use another piece of paper.

13. Now for each one pick one or two positive responses from your list and let that soak in for a minute.

14. Why does negativity have a need to feed?

15. What are the three mental phases that the mind goes through in the skit?

16. When Mr. Thorp starts to explain to the family about negative character phrases which phase does Mr. Johnson end up in and acts on?

17. Because Mr. Johnson had a need to feed his negativity whose negative character weaknesses is expose?

18. Which phase does Mrs. Johnson end up in competing for the loudest voice?

19. What is Mr. Thorp really trying to do?

20. Explain what yelling accomplishes in your own words.

21. Does someone yelling at you make you feel good inside?

22. Yelling at people can expose open mental wounds that have never healed causing mental warfare between, which phases.

23. When Mr. Thorp attempts to educate the family about contributing to ticking time bombs Mr. Johnson expresses which negative character weakness?

24. What do you think starts to build in Matt when his parents yell at him?

25. What mistakes are Matt's parents making by assuming that Matt is quiet?

26. When the mind goes in and out of mental combat, do you think he or she is aware of it at the time? Yes or no.

27. If you are a parent, do you think you can handle your child telling you, the truth about how they feel you handle situations and that they may be causing future mental combat in their minds? Yes or no.

28. If you answered yes, would you secretly hold it against them for helping educate you about a negative character weakness that you help create in them?

29. Is it a good time to talk about negative character weaknesses while they are young or when they get in their teenage years?

30. If you decide to ask your kids about their negative character weaknesses, what should you remember?

31. In order for good thoughts to emerge on a regular basis, you must?

32. What was the real cause that influenced Matt to want to beat up Tim?

33. Why did Matt not know why he wanted to beat up Tim?

34. Why is it important for the parents of Matt to know why their son had negative character weaknesses?

35. Do you think that when Matt say's do, I really have to answer that, that he may be agreeing with Mr. Thorp or thinking about something else like when him and Sam can go play outside?

36. Why does Matt tell his parents that he feels uncomfortable talking to them about anything?

37. Can parents discipline their children without yelling at them? Yes or no.

38. What does Mr. Thorp suggest the family do to better their situation?

39. Why would telling each other every day I appreciate you help after knowing the why?

40. What are the lists that Mr. Thorp tells the family to make?

41. What do negative character weaknesses do to a person in their life story?

42. What do you think happened when Mr. Johnson went into denial about the things Mr. Thorp was telling him about his son Matt?

43. What do you think is the reason why Sam was bold enough to defend Mr. Thorp?

44. Now that Sam has a better understanding of the reason, why people do what they do; does he have to agree with what his parents think? Yes or no.

45. As problems and situations expose the negative character weaknesses in Sam's life, what does he do as a result?

46. Why do you think Sam and his family are competing?

47. How does Sam describe how he still wins, if he loses the competition?

48. When Mr. Johnson gets to work what does his coworker Fred say to him?

49. Why does Fred say I appreciate you to Mr. Johnson?

50. What does Mr. Johnson do when Fred explains the why he appreciated him? This is in your own words.

51. What happen to Fred when he tried to reach out to his son when he got older?

52. What helped Fred with the problems he was having with his son?

53. What advice did Fred give Matt Sr.? In your own words.

54. What mistake did Fred make when disciplining his son? In your own words

55. What was fueling the mental warfare going on in Fred sons mind?

56. Why does Mrs. Ringer ask Mrs. Johnson why she replied with I appreciate you in return to what Mrs. Ringer said?

57. Was Mrs. Johnson's appreciation the same as Mrs. Ringers and why not?

58. What was one mistake Sam's parents made raising Sam?

59. When Mrs. Ringer gave Mrs. Johnson advice about her son, what negative character weaknesses do you think were exposed in Mrs. Johnson?

60. What does Mrs. Ringer suggest that the Johnson family do to help them?

61. Why do you think Mrs. Johnson did not have to worry about asking Matt to admit what is wrong with him?

62. Will this technique answer the *why* questions that engage in a person's mind? Yes or no.

63. What is a good way to purge out the negative weaknesses in the heart?

64. Where are the negative character weaknesses stored after they leave the heart?

65. What does Mrs. Ringer say is the best thing that you get out of doing the program?

66. What did it take for Mrs. Ringer to go over to her friend's house and explain how their family relationship improved?

67. When Matt and Sam met their friends, do you think that Sam has any idea about mental warfare that is going on in Scott's mind? Yes or no.

68. How does Scott respond when Sam tells him I appreciate you in front of everybody?

69. Why does Sam not get angry with Scott for being smart in front of everybody?

70. How does Sam start to balance Scott's need to feed his negativity?

71. What did Scott say when Sam complimented him?

72. Why did Sam say, your parents yelling at you is only part of the problem?

73. How was Sam able to breakdown to Scott the mental warfare going on in his mind when he was not there?

SCENCE SIX

Narrator: This skit shows Matt and Sam reflecting at a young age exposing things that they and their parents did not take seriously. Matt and Sam are over Sam's house hanging out.

Matt: I remember when I was 6 years old.

Narrator: Matt starts to talk about what happen to him. Then Sam tells Matt what happen to him at 6 years old. At 6 years old, Matt's father offers him a puff of his cigarette. Matt sees how cool his father looks smoking his cigarette, which starts the mental warfare going on in his mind. After Matt takes a puff, he asks for another one and his father says, no get away from me!

Narrator: In addition, he starts laughing. Matt and his father were oblivious to the mental warfare going on in Matt's mind.

Narrator: In Matt's mind, he first struggles with the situation of his father offering him a puff of his cigarette.

Narrator: Matt at that age is too young and lacks understanding to turn it down, plus he looks up to his father.

Narrator: Matt's father was drinking beer and smoking, while he was watching TV and not thinking about how it would affect his son later on in life.

Narrator: Matt's father never considered the long-term mental affect that he imposed on Matt at a young age that would affect his choices in society...

Narrator: The warfare going on in Matt's mind started with: desire, coveting, fear, sensitivity, hurt, anger, impatience, disrespect, rebellion, grudge and then resentment.

Narrator: In this case, Matt's initial problem is desire. Desire, coupled with coveting, wins the mental battle; which causes a void that needs attention and to be filled.

Narrator: Matt felt resentment in his life every time a person resembles someone yelling at him, getting smart with him, and telling him he cannot have what he wants.

Narrator: This leads to the need to feed his negativity while he is very oblivious to it. This also is the why Matt continues to get into trouble at a young age.

Narrator: Matt has held a grudge and resentment for his father for at least 12 years without his father knowing it now that he is 18 years old.

Narrator: Since he was much younger, Matt has experienced the negative character weaknesses: Holding a grudge and resentment, along with various other weaknesses.

Narrator: But Matt did not know this or how to communicate it to anyone. He had a fear of retaliation from his father in his mind.

Narrator: To make matters worse Matt's father thinks that just because Matt is quiet when he yells at him, that he is being respectful.

Narrator: When in reality Matt's father is influencing Matt to build on the walls of holding a grudge and resentment.

Narrator: Please understand that even though the initial negative character weaknesses of desire and coveting may have had the loudest voice now, resentment continues to build forces in the background.

Narrator: The various environments Matt is introduced to in some way reinforces Matt's need to feed his negativity.

Narrator: This is because Matt seeks out the negative character weaknesses in whomever, and will exploit them to his advantage.

Narrator: By doing this, Matt pleases his negative character weaknesses for the moment.

Narrator: Some parents do not think much of what they were doing while allowing their kids to see and experience things, because they think it is cute or funny.

Narrator: It's possible that they felt that at that time it was no big deal.

Narrator: The skit changes scenes to a scene inside a brain displaying the mental warfare going on in Matt's brain.

Narrator: People walk around wrestling each other to see who has the loudest voice.

Narrator: There are words displaying negative character weaknesses on the front and back of the people representing the mental battle going on in his brain.

Narrator: The people take turns shouting out their esoteric negative/regular negative character weaknesses while wrestling.

Narrator: At the end of the battle desire comes in and the last negative character weakness that wins the battle shouts out with desire all together.

Desire: As an example: Desire shouts out "I desire"

Covet: Covet shouts out "to covet what you have"

Narrator: They shout these saying about 3 times.

Narrator: The scene changes back to Matt and Sam at Sam's house.

Sam: When I was 6, I remember hearing my grandmother say to both of my parents, only the best for my grandkids.

Narrator: Since Sam came from a rich family, he figured that he could get whatever he wanted when he wanted since he heard his grandmother talking to his parents.

Narrator: What Sam did not know or hear is his grandmother talking about her wanting her grandkids to attend the best schools.

Narrator: Sam only heard what he wanted to hear even though he was in the same room that they were talking in.

Narrator: Sam did not do that on purpose, he was oblivious to what was going on in his mind.

Narrator: After that scene, the scene changes to Sam talking about another time at six when his family was in a department store shopping.

Narrator: Sam tells his parents he wants a certain cell phone.

Narrator: All Sam knows and remembers in his mind is he heard his grandmother say only the best for my grandkids.

Narrator: Sam's parents explained to Sam that the cell phone he wanted cost too much money.

Narrator: Sam's parents are oblivious as to the fact that Sam only heard part of the conversation that his parents had with his grandparents.

Narrator: The parents are also oblivious to the mental warfare going on in Sam's mind.

Narrator: The scene changes to a fight going on in Sam's mind.

Narrator: People display signs of each esoteric negative/regular negative character weakness going on in his mind while fighting.

Narrator: Sam's negative character weaknesses start out with; anger, selfishness, sensitivity, resentment, and disrespect.

Narrator: Disrespect wins the battle of the loudest voice.

Narrator: Then the scene shows desire come in saying,

Desire: I desire.

Narrator: In addition, the negative character weakness of disrespect says,

Disrespect: I desire disrespect.

Narrator: They both say it 3 times.

Sam: You know I held a grudge against my parents for 5 years.

Sam: I see now why I did; it was that need to feed my negativity.

Narrator: Sam held a grudge against his parents, because when he was 13 his father said just before he pulled him out of private school into public school; why can't you be like us staying out of trouble and doing what you are told?

Sam: I answered disrespectfully than as well, because my negative character weakness of disrespect had the loudest voice.

Narrator: While all this is going on Sam is reflecting on the other negative character weaknesses in the background that lost the battle, but were building up inside.

Sam: When we got home my mom asked me why I acted so disrespectfully at the store.

Narrator: That question exposed Sam's negative character weakness of denial.

Narrator: As Sam and Matt were reflecting on their life after learning from Mr. Thorp, they could remember when some of the negative character weaknesses started.

Narrator: They also could remember the times when their negative character weaknesses had the need the feed.

Narrator: This skit displays a visual idea of some of the mental warfare that occurs in the mind.

Narrator: This skit shows you how the book The Revelation of Why applies in a visual sense.

Narrator: This skit demonstrates how a child may process how you deal with them and the mental baggage that can come from it.

Narrator: This skit displays a possible thought of a child hearing the wrong thing, acting on it and activating negative character weaknesses that the parents are very unaware of although the child was in the same room.

Narrator: As parents, we must be mindful about who and what we say in front of children, especially if it does not pertain to them.

Narrator: The skit makes a point about Sam and Matt-processing times in the past where they were able to recognize the starting point of their negative character weaknesses.

Narrator: Matt and Sam both realized that the negative character weakness with the loudest voice with desire may get most of the attention.

Narrator: The other ones that lost the battle are still their just lying dormant for the next person, problem, or situation to expose them.

Narrator: We also saw in the skit that desire does not necessarily have to be last; it could be first as well.

Narrator: The reason why desire has a big voice is that without it, it would be hard to act on whatever negative character weakness has the loudest voice.

Narrator: Matt realizes that before he developed his addiction to cigarettes now, he first had to have the desire with coveting already lying dormant in him waiting to be exposed.

Narrator: Now Matt understands the reason why he talks to his friend Sam and others the way he does.

Narrator: Both Matt and Sam both recognize now why they do what they do and can now help other people move forward in life by using the techniques in The Revelation of Why.

Scene Seven

Narrator: In this skit, Matt and Sam are in one environment.

Narrator: The first environment is at a barbecue.

Narrator: Matt and Sam go into the house.

Sam: Let's see if we can help any of our friends with their mental combat.

Matt: Yeah, let's see who is having a need to feed their negativity.

Narrator: Their friend John walks up to them and says,

John: Hey guys "what's up?"

Sam: I can't call it.

Matt: What's up with you?

John: I can't stand the way Jennifer laughs, what about you?

Narrator: Matt and Sam both look at each other and shake their head.

John: Why did you look at each other like that?

Sam: I appreciate you.

Matt: I appreciate you as well.

John: Why, what did I do, is that why you looked at each other.

Sam: Yes.

John: I appreciate you too.

Sam: Why do you appreciate us?

John: Ah, because you guys are cool.

Sam: We appreciate you for you being you, not for what you did or for what you're going to do

Sam: Can you argue with that.

John: I cannot argue with that point.

Sam: There's nothing wrong with what you said,

Sam: The difference is you might not make me happy tomorrow, but I still will appreciate you for you being you.

Sam: Although I might dislike the tactics of my enemy, I can appreciate the lessons that better prepare me for the next battle, whatever it may be.

Sam: My appreciation is non-conditional.

Sam: We are working on our positive character traits can you help us with that?

John: Sure, what do I have to do?

Sam: Just try to beat us telling you we appreciate you before you tell us the same thing.

Sam: That way we all get instant celebrity status for not doing anything special.

Sam: Watch and see if you do not notice a difference in how people respond back to you if they know up front the why you are appreciating them.

John: Sure, I'll do it.

John: Where ever you got that from, it's a good way to make a person feel good and wanted.

Sam: We got it from a man named Mr. Thorp.

Sam: If you never got past the why and you were for example corrected for something that you feel that you shouldn't have been corrected.

Sam: If our feelings for being corrected haven't been addressed on a daily basis you might be a ticking time bomb waiting for someone to expose that negative character weakness in that environment.

Sam: This starts the mental warfare that goes on in your mind.

Sam: Is there anything that you can think of that you still hold inside from childhood that you have not let go or received any mental relief?

John: Yes.

John: I never got over how my parents favored my older brother.

John: That's why I don't get along with my brother or my parents.

Sam: I want to let you know that I care about you and what you think

John: Thanks man, nobody has ever told me that.

Sam: Did you ever wonder why you keep making bad choices?

John: I never thought about it, but now that you mention it, it's something to think about.

Sam: Our negative character weaknesses are tested everyday several times a day.

Sam: What do you think is fueling the negative thoughts that enter your mind?

John: I don't know, whatever is upsetting me at the time, I guess.

Sam: We found out that it's our negative character weaknesses that have a need to feed our negativity.

John: Really, that's interesting.

John: I never thought about it like that.

Sam: Did you agree with everything that we just said?

John: Yeah, why.

Sam: Because you are now an eye witness to how we saw how you were in need to feed your negative character weaknesses.

John: What do you mean?"

Sam: You agreed that me appreciating you was different, but made you feel wanted or cared about, right?'

Sam: When you started talking about our friend Jennifer too, we knew that you were in need to feed your negative character weaknesses.

Sam: We worked on our positive character trait which was not complimenting people enough to stop you from exposing our negative character weaknesses.

Sam: When you get the book The Revelation of Why and learn what to do then you can sit back and observe why people do what they do.

QUESTIONS

In this Workbook you will take a step deeper into the Revelation of Why. We will reveal a reflection of Matt and Sam's childhood past that will shine some light on helping you realize why they are partly the way they are. This work book will possibly help you be able to remember some things that happen to you in your past that you may have forgotten or just have not dealt with. After coming to the realization of where your negative character weaknesses come from maybe you can use some of this knowledge to work on yours as well.

1. At the age of six what was Matt and Sam reflecting on?

2. What happens to Matt at six?

3. What was wrong with Matt's offer to have a cigarette at six?

4. What starts the mental warfare going on in Matt's mind?

5. List the mental combat that was going on in Matt's mind at six.

6. Which two negative character weaknesses do Matt start out with at first?

7. What would expose Matt's resentment in life?

8. What would Matt have to do to continue to feel negative?

9. Is Matt aware of the fact that he has to feed the need to be negative?

10. How long has Matt held a grudge on his father?

11. Did Matt's negative character weaknesses start at six?

12. What did Matt's father do by yelling at Matt?

13. Was Matt's father aware of the mental warfare going on in Matt's mind?

14. Although Desire and coveting had the loudest voice what was building in the background?

15. What was Sam's first recollection at age six?

16. Did Sam hear everything that his grandmother said to his parents?

17. What did Sam not hear his grandmother say?

18. 18.Did Sam place limitations in his mind as to what he wanted to hear and focused on what he wanted to know?

19. Did Sam do it on purpose?

20. What exposed the mental warfare going in Sam's mind?

21. Were Sam's parents aware of the mental warfare going on in Sam's mind?

22. Name at least 9 negative character weaknesses you observed.

23. Which negative character weaknesses had the loudest voice?

24. How long did Sam hold a grudge against his parents?

25. Did Sam realize why he held a grudge for 5 years?

26. Why did Sam say he held a grudge for 5 years?

27. Why did Sam answer his father disrespectfully?

28. Which negative character weakness did his mother expose in him when they got home from the store?

29. What happen to Sam when he was 13 years old?

30. What did Matt and Sam plan to use to help them stop other people's negative character weaknesses from exposing theirs?

ANSWERS

1. Esoteric
2. The tone of voice, correction, sensitivity, and resentment
3. Resentment
4. I exercised control and restraint.
5. Disrespect, pride, impatience
6. Denial
7. Manifesting calm and patience taking deep breathes turning the focus off the cast member or problem and recognizing your weakness and accepting the problem. Recognizing your weaknesses and accepting the fact that they are oblivious to the need to feed and the testing of character.
8. Anger, frustration, impatience, disrespect, no tolerance, and resentment.
9. Anger, frustration, wrath, hatred, fear, impatience, lying, disrespect, cussing and resentment.
10. Disappointment, impatience
11. Being honest telling the truth even when no one was around to witness what you done.

12. Because he had a need to feed his negativity.
13. Anger, rage, strife, corrupt mind, fault finding, short fuse, boredom, and desire.
14. You do not tell me what to do; you do as I say and what I tell you to do.
15. Pick from your list
16. Tone of voice, correction, sensitivity, and resentment.
17. Pick from your list.
18. Pick from your list.
19. Pick from your list.

ANSWERS

1. Limitations on what subject Sam was going to talk about, how long Matt was going to entertain what Sam had to say and if he should even believe Sam.
2. For you being you, not for what you did or what you are going to do.
3. Each of the family members had conditions on their appreciation for Mr. Thorp, but his does not have any conditions. This is to bring out the fact that you should accept a person for who they are and not what they did or going to do, because tomorrow you may not be in the best of moods. If you are not in the best of moods still appreciate someone anyway.
4. Esoteric negative/ regular negative character weaknesses.
5. About the origin from where what influences our thoughts comes from and to show you a way to combat some of the ticking time bombs walking around ready to go off at a moment's notice to defend their thoughts in a negative way.

6. Mental warfare that is in a battle to see who has the loudest voice to influence your thoughts.

7. Lack of trust, fear, disappointment, anger, fault finding and short fuse.

8. You must use a positive response.

9. It is the process by, which you make a conscious effort on a daily basis all day long, not so much to focus on the people or problems, but on your inner self at the time, you are thoughts begin to experience negativity.

10. Private, hidden or concealed.

11. In your own words.

12. In your own words.

13. From your own list.

14. In order to survive.

15. Esoteric, regular negative and negative character weakness phrases.

16. The negative character weakness phrase.

17. Mrs. Johnson.

18. The negative character weakness phrase.

19. He is trying to educate people who may not realize how they are contributing to the ticking time bombs waiting to go off at a moment's notice to defend their thoughts in a negative way.

20. In your own words.

21. In your own words.

22. Esoteric negative, regular negative character weakness and negative character weakness phrases

23. Denial.

24. Resentment.

25. That he will respect her when he gets older.

26. No.

27. You answer yes or no.

28. You answer in your own words.

29. You make those decisions. Only you know how fast your child is maturing.

30. You should remember that they are very sensitive and you do not need to ignite any mental warfare. Make them feel as comfortable as possible.

31. Purge the heart that feed the subconscious.

32. Correction, which started from his younger days.

33. This is because as the mind exist the esoteric phase and enters the regular negative character weakness phase it forgets about the old war and focuses on the new one at hand.

34. It is important for Mr. Johnson to know about matt's negative character weakness, because later on in life when he calls his self-reaching out to him trying to make a stronger bond, he will still hold resentment and you will wonder why.

35. Agreeing with Mr. Thorp

36. Because they yell at him so much.

37. Yes

38. Mr. Thorp suggests that they start telling each other I appreciate you every day.

39. This would help build excitement every day to try to be the first to say I appreciate you. Just knowing that you are accepting me for who I am and not for what I did or going to do, tells me that even when I do wrong and you discipline me, I know you still appreciate me and vice versa.

40. Esoteric negative/ regular negative character weakness list, negative character weakness phrase list, positive response list, positive traits list, fun mental release response list. You must make a list of negative character weakness in all your environments, then a list of which one you adopted in those environments. Make a list comparing the list of adopted negative character weaknesses to your original one to see which environment has the need to feed your negativity.

41. It places limitation on who they will talk to, how long they are willing to entertain what a person has to say, how far they will go in life and if happiness is even an option.

42. Mr. Johnson placed limitations on Mr. Thorp as to his credibility; even though all he was trying to do was help him become aware of the potential mental warfare that may lie dormant waiting to go off in his son.

43. Because Sam could testify to the changes, he saw in his family having the confidence to be able to talk to

his parents about anything and not feel as if he does not matter and less of a person.

44. No

45. Sam does not focus on the person, problem, or situation; but ask his self, which negative character weaknesses, is being exposed, so I can eliminate the potential mental warfare that might begin if I give into it.

46. To see who has the most points, have fun and rebuild to better a dysfunctional family relationship.

47. By his whole family working on themselves individually and keeping a log, he can see which negative character weaknesses his parents are working on. This helps them improve a positive character trait called trust.

48. I appreciate you.

49. Fred tells Mr. Johnson I appreciate you for you being you, not for what he did or what you're going to do.

50. In your own words.

51. Fred's son would abuse him and have no remorse.

52. In your own words.

53. In your own words.

54. In your own words.

55. His need to feed his negativity.

56. She did it to see if Mrs. Johnson knew the understanding, of the why I appreciate you without conditions on it.

57. In your own words.

58. They thought that pressuring Sam into being what they wanted Sam to be would make them and Sam happy, instead it built up a mental wall of concealed resentment.

59. Short fuse, impatience, anger, and denial only for a brief moment.

60. She suggests that the whole family try the program together.

61. Because she can look in the book and see, which negative character weaknesses, he is working on.

62. No

63. To encourage one another daily and chose as many positive character responses as you can to build points and deal with problems.

64. In the subconscious

65. Whether you win or lose you are competing for points and growing towards change in your life and your family's life, while helping minimize the ticking time bombs in the world.

66. In your own words.

67. No

68. With a smart answer.

69. Because Sam knows the why. Scott is in need to feed his negativity.

70. Sam tells Scott that I appreciate you for you and not what you did or what you are going to do.

71. That was the best encouragement I received in a long time.

72. Because negative character weakness plays a major role as well.

73. After reading the book The Revelation of Why he was able to figure out the why Scott does what does.

ANSWERS

1. SIX.
2. Matt's Dad offers him a cigarette.
3. Matt's too young and lacks understanding to turn it down, he looks up to his father, while matt's father was drinking and smoking, he wasn't thinking about how he talked to his son or treated him on a regular basis. Matt's father never thought about the long-term effects on his son later in life.
4. Matt's father offering him a cigarette at six.
5. Desire, coveting, fear, sensitivity, hurt, anger, impatience, disrespect, rebellion, grudge, and resentment.
6. Desire and coveting.
7. Every time someone resembles yelling at him, getting smart with him or telling him he cannot have what he wants.
8. Matt would have to feed his need to be negative.
9. No.
10. 12 years.
11. No.

12. Matt's father believes he was showing him respect, but in reality, he was influencing him to build on the walls of resentment and holding a grudge.

13. No.

14. Grudge and resentment.

15. Sam recalled hearing his grandmother telling his parents only the best for my grandkids.

16. No.

17. Sam did not hear his grandmother say to his parents, she wanted her grandkids to go to the best schools.

18. Yes.

19. No.

20. Sam was told that, he could not have a cell phone, because it cost too much money.

21. No

22. Anger, selfishness, resentment, hurt, rebellion, frustration, impatience, disrespect and desire.

23. Disrespect and desire.

24. 5 years.

25. Yes

26. Sam held a grudge for 5 years, because he had a need to feed his negativity.

27. Disrespect and desire had the loudest voice.

28. Denial

29. Sam father pulled him out of private school and told him why you cannot be like us staying out of trouble and doing what you are told.

30. The Revelation of Why

Recognizing Witnesses that observed me using my techniques either at the Rutherford County Jail or outside of it in the public.

- Former Lt. Terry Nicodemus – terrypck@yahoo.com
- Former Lt. Tara A. Corder – taraantoinette@bellsouth.net
- Booking Cpl. Randy Miller – randymiller319@gmail.com
- Detention St. Ja-Cal J. Johnson – jacaljohnson@gmail.com
- Patrol Deputy Thomas (T.J.) Hinson – thomashinson3@gmail.com
- Planet Fitness Rep. Mike Anderson – mike@pfoftn.com
- Deputy Chuck Sayler – sayler2527@gmail.com
- Dr. Victor Poletajev (Chiropractor) – myostar@aol.com
- Former Booking Deputy Haley Stone – Hstone501@gmail.com
- Detention Deputy Joel Jenkins – Jenkinsjoel17@yahoo.com

www.ingramcontent.com/pod-product-compliance
Lightning Source LLC
Chambersburg PA
CBHW071737120626
46550CB00002B/560